The Joy of C++ Programming

A Practical Guide

for

Zombies and the Undead

By

J. Burton Browning, Ed.D.

First Edition

2018

Wrongway Corrigan Farms Publishing

ISBN: 978-1-387-69048-0

Dedication

This book is dedicated to My dad, Hugh Burton Browning, Misibo Wrongway Corrigan, Champion Koblizec Pools of Azure of Misibo, Champion Gotier BoJangles of Misibo and Champion Suyaki Mama's Mia of Misbo. Dad, you were the best and I miss you. You taught me so much, touched so many lives, and lived a life only the best could hope to mirror. You made it through impossible adversity with grace. Wrongway and BoJangles, no one could have asked for better boys. You both set a super high standard that only a special friend could hope to meet. And to Azure and Mia, you were both so loving. Mia you were such a trooper and tough girl and the best momma-cat. I miss you all so much and will always have "two hands" for you. Love and purrs always,

Burton

Table of Contents

Chapter 1

How to use and IDE, basic data types, and the IF single selection structure

There are many different tools or development environments you could use to write and make functional a C++ program. You could use a text editor to write the code and a command-line compiler to convert the human-readable C++ code to something the computer can execute, machine language code (otherwise known as binary executable code). Or you could use a tool that integrates editor, debugger, compiler, etc. all into one neat package. Many support multiple languages so you only have to learn the tool once, then you can add on other languages, with their associated syntax, at a later time.

The benefits of a full-featured IDE (Integrated Development Environment) such as Microsoft Visual Studio, Netbeans, Eclipse, Dev C++, and many others bring features such as debugging (helping you find errors), version control (keep track of different editions or versions of your code), search and replace, color syntax highlighting (*key* or *reserved words* in the program are a different color for easy recognition by the programmer), and help menus, to name but a few of the features.

This text will work with any, but it will focus on Microsoft Visual Studio for consistency. It should also be noted that C++ is a cross-platform language in that within reason it can be recompiled for many different types of devices, but this text will focus on the IBM PC compatible platform (e.g. Windows/DOS). With all of this discussion about IDE's, let's get started with one you can download for free from Microsoft, Visual Studio (at least it was free as of early 2017 but due to M.S. seeing everything under the sun belongs to them (read "it is all a service" this is subject to change and beyond the scope of this text.

How to use Visual Studio

Visual Studio is an Integrated Development Environment (IDE) from Microsoft which is generic in that it supports multiple languages (such as C++, C#, VB.NET, etc.). The look and feel of the editor, debugger, and compiler are the same for all languages which it supports, which are many.

This was not the case with earlier versions, and certainly is not the case with special purpose IDE's from other sources such as Lazarus with is for open Delphi only. Now, depending on whether you download the Express version, the latest M.S. downloadable version, or you purchased a version you will have extra (or not!) features. However, for this text any freely available version of Visual Studio will be very similar as of 2017 Community Edition of Visual Studio.

Get started with Microsoft Visual Studio

1) After an install of Visual Studio from MSDN, Dreamspark, or wherever you obtained it, start the program. Certainly you can obtain the Express edition of Visual Studio with a quick web search as well. Note if you create an ISO (and image of a DVD disc) of Visual Studio you will need to either burn the ISO to a disc or you will need to mount the ISO as if it was a disc and install from that point. Double clicking the ISO will not allow you to install it! M.S. as of 2017 has made it such that you have to create an ISO, downloading is now not an option, but if you get a 2015 or older ISO that will work great, no worries.

2) On the main page, Under *Start* on the left select *New Project* (if starting a new one).

3) <u>Note</u> that at the bottom of the screen <u>it is critical that you must change to a location you can access</u>, such as a folder you can find, your pen drive, etc. Browse and do this and select *Empty project* and press OK.

To save to a "default" location of your choice using Visual Studio, try the following.

Here we assume we want to save all projects to a folder on the desktop named New Folder (a creative name!)

From Visual Studio select:

Tools

Options

Projects and Solutions

**Note you change the project location on the right via the browse button to where you want to save!

Name:	ConsoleApplication1		
Location:	c:\users\jbbrowning\documents\visual studio 2017\Projects	▾	Browse...
Solution name:	ConsoleApplication1		☑ Create directory for soluti
			☐ Add to Source Control
			OK

Image 1.1 Screen capture of Visual Studio project saving location.

4) In the project, right click on the folder to the right named *Source Files.*

5) Select *Add, New Item*, Select C++ File, and at the bottom give it a DOS style name with no spaces or wacky characters such as for HW problem #1 it might be *ch1_hw1.cpp*   Write the following code in the empty file. Then select File, Save All.

```
#include <iostream>

int main()
{
        std::cout << "Hello C++!!";  // note two colons between words
        system("pause");
        return 0;
}
```

6) When done, select *Debug Start Debugging* and *yes* to build. For now just type and run this, a discussion of each line will follow shortly.

7) *Hello* should display! This is the command line or CLI (Command Line Interface) and all of our programs for this text will be from the CLI. Press any key to close the window and return to the IDE. Now, that you have written your first C++ program, let's see what is going on under the hood a little bit.

First, line termination (or when you tell the compiler Visual Studio) you are done with a statement and want to have that complete statement processed, you end the line with a semi colon. This is important since your lines can span multiple lines, but still be one statement and are only processed after you type the semi color.

Check your zombie weapons

To see what happens when you leave a semi colon out, delete one from the aforementioned code and re-run it. Note the error. The debugger is trying to help you find "bugs" or errors in your code, sometimes it will get you close, sometimes not as it depends on the error.

Upper and lower case are important! You could also change the command to output to the console **cout** to be **Cout** and you would get an error. C++ is a case sensitive language, so be careful when typing.

Next, change your code to include the comments // which are notes only for you the programmer and are ignored by the compiler. There are **two types of comments**, *single line* which start with // and *multi-line* such as with /* and */

If you want to **comment out several lines at a time** you could use multi-line comments. It is also important to note that *spacing does not matter with C++ and tabbing lines and using white space between code is a matter of coding style which leads to readability*, which is very important.

cout

The command **cout** is and the associated indirection operators << allow you to output to the computer screen or *console* from your program. Think *Console OUTput* and the indirection "alligators" point to where you want the data to go to. So, if you had **cout << "crossbow"** the string data "crossbow" would point to the *cout* or send the string "crossbow" to the console. Consider the following which has a multiline comment:

```
#include <iostream> // include a library of pre-written code
using namespace std; /* this includes "basic functions in iostream  such as cout, cin, etc
        which are in the library you just included and allows you to not need a fully qualified
name such as std::cout.....much easier right? */

int main()  // You will always have one and only one main functions to drive the program
{      // braces must be on the very next line with no spaces inbetween...if you have a
        //left you much close with a right brace (but you knew that from Math 101!!)  The
         //int represents a data type (variable) that will be returned to main, which will be 0 if
        //it runs properly.
        cout << "Hello C++!!\n";    // note we did not have to use std::
        // also note  /n is a new line literal and causes the cursor to move
        //done one line on the output screen...and /a is system bell.  Turn your speakers
```

```
//up and try it.
//try several /a/a/a  for three beeps, etc.
system("pause");  // You can run Windows system commands such as pause to hold a
                        //window open.  However any valid system command works.
return 0;  // this is returned to main and the program ends!
}
```

When finished, run this as you did in step 6 above.

Program control

So, we will return to this later, but there are basically only **three types of control structures in any computer program** and you have just learned about one, **sequence**. The *sequence structure starts from the first line of code and moves down to the last, with no changes or branches off to other areas*. The program you just wrote started at the top and moved down line by line executing one line of code after the other. The other two types of control structures are selection structures (*if* statements) and looping structures (*while* and *for*). More on these later.

Key to note is that we used extensive comments to leave ourselves notes about what is going on and to make our code a bit "self documenting" so that someone unfamiliar with it could read it. Next we used a process of cyclical refinement to improve our program. You got it to run, then you went back and made improvements (such as adding in using namespace std to eliminate the need for *std::* in front of *cout*. You also learned a bit about escape sequences, which is exactly what the \n and \a are. They actually do something instead of being displayed. There are more of them, but let's save further discussion on this for later.

Lastly, this thing called a compiler was mentioned. Your IDE combines several tools to allow you to write programs. In short you have an editor which allows you to write your code. When you run your code, several things go on in the background. The a parser and lexical analyzer program "reads" your code for keywords (reserved words) that actually do something (such as *cout*) and tries to interpret what you want the program code to do. The Linker takes that header file you included, which is actually a separate file with a great deal more C++ code, and includes that with your code to make a much later object file with all the code. A compiler takes the object code and converts it to machine-specific binary code with can be executed on the platform you are building for. Whew! A great deal is going on behind the scenes when you click run!!!

More revision on the first program

Next let's try a minor variation. In this next example you can see two system commands, in this case a direction DOS command run as well. Look up DOS commands online and try some others. Do note though this is Windows specific so will not work on Linux, Mac, etc. Writing code to include the system command will generally make your code not portable to other platforms.

```
#include <iostream>
using namespace std;

int main()
{
        cout << "These are files and folders in the directory where\n";

        system("dir");  // DOS command to show a directory listing  dir/w and dir/p are wide
        // and one page at a time respectively or you could show only

        system("pause");
        return 0;
}
```

Where is this executable binary file to be found?

If you are not careful, trying to find the binary file can be like trying to find crossbow bolts when a zombie horde is after you. The key is to note (and remember) where you created your solution when you first started your Visual Studio project. This cannot be stressed enough, *know where you created your solution and be able to navigate to it on the computer*!!!! So, we have been talking about the exe or executable file, but where is it created if you wanted to copy it and give it to someone (who would not need Visual Studio to run it and could just run it as any normal program)?

By default with Visual Studio places projects in the My Documents Visual Studio folder, unless you specify another location, which is the best idea. Look in Visual Studio (and the year of your version) then Projects, then your project folder. Open the folder for the project you created. In the folder will be a Debug folder, once you have successfully built your project. Open that folder and you will see an executable (this file has an *.exe extension) you can copy and distribute to users and other zombie hunters. If you are still lost on finding your files (and you shouldn't be) open your project, then to the right in Visual Studio under the Solution explorer, right click on the project and note that at the bottom of the dropdown list, you will see an option to open the folder....containing your project files!

Working with Variables

As it happens, in some languages, such as *strongly typed languages* you have to declare each variable's type before you can use it. A non-strongly typed language is the opposite of this. To declare variables in C++ consider:

> float tax = .07;

where we declare a variable named tax to be a float, and hold an initial value of .07

As of C++ 14 things changed a bit about declaring a variables type such that the compiler will determine it for you, but not at run-time, but during compile time (which still makes C++ a strongly typed language). Basically the number is the year the International Standards Organization -- ISO, approved changes to the syntax of the language. The *auto* keyword allows this to take place. Consider the following code:

```
#include <iostream>
using namespace std;

int main()
{
        auto what_number = 3.14;
        cout << "This was the number: " << what_number << endl;
        system("pause");
        return 0;
}
```

Again, with a *non-strongly typed language* a variables type is automatically determined by the type of data stored in it. Python and Visual Basic.NET (when Option Explicit is off) are two examples of non-strongly typed languages. However there are many different opinions on how to define this in the programming world, others refer to *strongly typed* as *statically typed* so certainly it is prudent to take the definitions as a guide only, with regards to how other professionals will refer to the topic. Then *endl* (think *end l*ine) is the same as a "*\n*" and pushes the cursor to the next line. Now let's talk about data types and variables.

Types of data types and variables

Since data is stored in computer memory, it stands to reason that the area saved to store that data must be of the appropriate size to hold the data you plan to store since computers have a finite amount of memory available for this use (as the OS and other things all need to use this RAM as well). That being said, there are many variable data types C++ can store. Each has a unique name, type (size), and value. Consider these primitive types which are available, characters, whole numbers, boolean data, and floating point numbers. *Strings* are a data type as well, but since *strings* are groups of characters we will consider them separately. First we will examine *characters*.

Characters

Based on your character encoding set (such as ASCII (American Standard Code for Information Interchange which supports only 256 characters) the *char* data type will fill many of your needs. However, there are larger character types which support international characters. They are:

char -- one byte in size, 8 bits.

char16_t -- 16 bits.

char32_t -- 32 bits.

wchar_t -- supports the international character set and is larger than the aforementioned types.

If you need Western European fonts, etc. UTF 8, UTF16, or UTF32 hold more data respectively to represent them so use a larger character type such as char16_t or larger. Consider the following code example to see how they work.

```
#include <iostream>
using namespace std;

int main()
{
        char a1 = 'a';  // 256 all positive  values
```

```cpp
        unsigned char b1 = 100;  // 0 to 127 range

        char NameA = ' '; // ASCII space
        char NameB = 32;  //ASCII decimal for space is 32

        cout << "Fun with chars!" << endl;

        cout << a1 << "   " << b1 << endl << " | " << NameA << "=" << NameB << " | " <<
        "Both space and 32 ASCII are same!" << endl;

        system("pause");
        return 0;
}
```

Note that when using characters, a single quote is used on either side, versus double quotes for string data. Some languages go either way, but for consistency consider single for single characters and double quotes for more than one (string data).

Each data element (printable or not) is represented by a decimal value, such as ASCII value 32 for a space bar, in the ASCII table. Use a search engine to find ASCII table or try the following URL to see them: http://ascii.cl/ or http://www.theasciicode.com.ar/ascii-printable-characters/grave-accent-ascii-code-96.html Try the following to see it in action again.

```cpp
#include <iostream>
using namespace std;

int main()
{
        char NameC = 'Z'; // ASCII Z  ombie!!!!!
        char NameD = 90;  //ASCII decimal for Z is 90

        cout << endl << " >>> "<< NameC << " = " << NameD << " <<< " << endl;

        system("pause");
        return 0;
}
```

Next we will see how to handle whole number data.

Whole number integer data

Whole numbers or *integers* are numeric values which do not have a fractional value. So, integers might be 1, 5, 1000, etc. A fractional value such as 1.456 will be represented by floating point data types. Integers will come in very handy, so let's examine some of the different types and sizes of ***integers***.

Signed integers have a negative or positive (implied) sign, so if you had say a hypothetical integer of size 100, basically half would be negative -50 up and half would be positive, 50 down for a grade total of a size of 100. *Unsigned would be all positive*, e.g. up to 100 positive. So it is easy to choose signed or not depending on what your program is doing. If only counting up, perhaps unsigned is a better choice.

Signed integers

signed short int   –32,768 to 32,767

signed int –2,147,483,648 to 2,147,483,647

signed long int -- 32 bit –2,147,483,648 to 2,147,483,647

signed long long int -- 64 bit –9,223,372,036,854,775,808 to 9,223,372,036,854,775,807

Unsigned integers

unsigned short int 0 to 65,535

unsigned int 0 to 4,294,967,295

unsigned long int 0 to 4,294,967,295

unsigned long long int 0 to 18,446,744,073,709,551,615

Try the following two examples, which also demonstrate the *sizeof()* operator to see how **signed** and **unsigned integers** are declared, and check their byte size.

```
//Different data types and byte size using sizeof operator on signed integers
#include <iostream>
using namespace std;

int main()
{

        cout << "Here are some data types and their byte size" << endl;
```

```cpp
        cout << "Signed integers" << endl;
        cout << "------------------" << endl;
        signed short int ssi = 10;
        cout << ssi  << " is the value of variable ssi a signed short int negative 32,768 to 32,767"
<< endl;
        cout << sizeof(ssi) << " is the byte size of a signed short integer\n" << endl;

        signed int si = 1000;
        cout << si << " is the value of variable si a signed int neg. 2,147,483,648 to
2,147,483,647" << endl;
        cout << sizeof(si) << " is the byte size of a signed integer\n" << endl;

        signed long int sli = 10000;
        cout << sli << "is the value of variable sli a signed long int neg. 2,147,483,648 to
2,147,483,647" << endl;
        cout << "It is related to the bit-size of the computer how a long is represented, but it is
generally" << endl;
        cout << " short = 16 bit, int 16-32, and long 32." << endl;
        cout << sizeof(sli) << " is the byte size of a signed long integer 32 bit\n" << endl;

        signed long long int slli = 100000;
        cout << slli << "is the value of variable slli a signed long long int neg.
9,223,372,036,854,775,808 to 9,223,372,036,854,775,807" << endl;
        cout << sizeof(slli) << " is the byte size of a signed long long integer 64 bit\n";

        system("pause");
        return 0;
}
```

Next let's look at unsigned integers.

```cpp
//Different data types and byte size using sizeof operator on unsigned integers
#include <iostream>
using namespace std;

int main()
{

        cout << "Here are some data types and their byte size" << endl;
        cout << "Unsigned integers" << endl;
        cout << "------------------" << endl;

        unsigned short int usi = 20;
        cout << usi << "is the value of variable usi = 0 to 4,294,967,295" << endl;
        cout << sizeof(usi) << " is the byte size of an unsigned short integer\n" << endl;
```

```
        unsigned int ui = 200;
        cout << ui << "is the value of variable ui = 0 to 65,535;" << endl;
        cout << sizeof(ui) << " is the byte size of an unsigned integer\n" << endl;

        unsigned long int uli = 2000;
        cout << uli << "is the value of variable uli = 0 to 4,294,967,295\n" << endl;
        cout << sizeof(uli) << " is the byte size of an unsigned long integer\n" << endl;

        unsigned long long int ulli = 200000;
        cout << ulli << "is the value of variable ulli = 0 to 18,446,744,073,709,551,615\n" <<
endl;
        cout << sizeof(ulli) << " is the byte size of an unsigned long long integer\n" << endl;

        cout << "Now it is time to shoot some zombies!!!\a\a\n";

        system("pause");
        return 0;
}
```

Now, it is interesting to note that if you tried to store a floating point value, such as 1.5 in an integer variable, it would store it...sort of. The fractional part will be truncated or dropped, and the whole number part will be stored. What you learned in Math 101 will not take place (e.g. it will not round to 2), so take important note of this!

```
//rounding
#include <iostream>
#include<cmath>
using namespace std;

int main()
{       cout << "Rounding!" << endl;

        cout << "=======================================" << endl;

        float n1 = 6.7;

        float n2 = 1.1;

        float n3 = 6.9;

        cout << (n1 + n2) << " <<< n1 added to n2" << endl;

        int result = n1 + n2;
```

```
        cout << result << " <<< bet you thought it would be 8 !!" << endl;

        float result2 = n1 + n2;

        // the next use the cmath library

        // round() rounds as you would expect

        cout << round(result2) << " <<< use round command in cmath library to round as we
were taught in math class"<<endl;   // this should be all one line

        //ceil() rounds up

        cout << ceil(result2) << " <<< use ceil to round up" << endl;

        //floor() rounds down

        cout << floor(result2) << " <<< use floor to round down" << endl;

        system("pause");

        return 0;

}
```

Floating point and boolean data types

So, if you have floating point data you will want to work with the float, double, and long double data types. The last, long double, will give the same precision on many hardware platforms as double, but basically a float will give you seven digits of precision and a double fifteen. Boolean data is for false and true or 0 for false and any positive integer for true. Use *bool* and a valid variable name to create boolean variables. The example below will give you an example of how floating point variable s and boolean variables work.

```
//Different float data types and byte size using sizeof operator
#include <iostream>
using namespace std;
#define PI 3.14159;

int main()
{
        cout << "Floating point and boolean data types" << endl;
        cout << "====================================" << endl;

        float my_float = 0;
```

16

```cpp
my_float = PI;

double my_double = PI;

long double my_long_double = PI;  // will be the same size as double when on Microsoft
    //compilers  other hardware may be different so sizeof is handy to check this!

bool my_bool = false;  // true or false 1 or 0 will all work

//cout.precision(50);
cout << my_float << " is the value stored in my_float" << endl;

cout << sizeof(my_float) << " is the byte size of my_float" << endl;

cout << my_double << " is my_double" << endl;

cout << sizeof(my_double) << " is the byte size" << endl;

cout << my_long_double << " is my_long_double" << endl;

cout << my_bool << " zero is false and any positive integer is true for boolean data" << endl;

system("pause");
return 0;    }
```

Naming variables

A variable is something whose value changes over time, that is stored in memory, and can be referenced by a nickname instead of the actual memory address. A game score, character points, a tax rate, or a last name might all be examples of potential variables. A variable has a name, type, size, and value.

That is a short and sweet definition of a variable, but let's move on. Naming variables can help in many respects such as program readability (by other programmers) and debugging. Good variable names set mediocre programmers apart from great programmers.

When you try the application which follows the variables could change every time you run the program. We declared them, which is required of C/C++. Since C++ is a **strongly typed language**, you must declare a variables *type* and *size* (e.g. tell the computer that MPG is an integer or whole-number data type. Additionally you might have to also give it an **initial value**, however this depends on the language. The *size* is implied, in part, based on the data type e.g. a

17

short int(eger) or long int(eger) or much larger a floating point value. Note that the names are in lower case and they do not have spaces in the name. Below are some valid and non-valid variable names.

Camel case versus snake case

It sounds like a great budget horror flick name, but in reality you can name your variables two different ways, with *camel case* or *snake case*. *Camel case* names have a capital letter or "hump" between the words, such as taxRate or sumOfNumbers, etc. *Snake case* has an underscore between keywords such as tax_rate or sum_of_numbers. Either will work with C or C++.

Valid:

firstName   lastName   itemsPurchased   number_of_dogs   gasPrice

gallonsUsedPerMonth

Non-valid:

&firstName   3gasprices   tax rategallonsusedtoday

lastname   x

* *lastname* and *x* would work and are valid but are not "good" names as far as being descriptive!

Also, to help make your programs more readable, you may want to add a comment statement after each variable declaration such as: int tax_rate =3; // this is the tax rate

```
//Variables
#include <iostream>
using namespace std;

int main()
{
        int n1 = 0;  // describe variable if needed
        int number_two = 0;    // snake case
        int numberThree = 0;  // camel case
        int sum = 0;  // no wacky characters such as $tax  89tax   tax value

        cout << "Enter first num:>  ";

        cin >> n1;
```

18

```cpp
        cout << "Enter second num:>  ";
        cin >> number_two;

        cout << "Enter third num:>  ";
        cin >> numberThree;

        sum = n1 + number_two + numberThree;

        cout << "and your sum is: " << sum  << "\n\a";

        system("pause");
        return 0;
}
```

Try the following second example with different types of variable names.

```cpp
//Another sample program with dif. types of variable names
#include <iostream>
using namespace std;

int main()
{
        float total = 0;
        int quantitySold = 0;
        float item_total = 0;
        float tax = 0;

        cout << "Enter item cost (each):>  ";
        cin >> item_total;
        cout << "Enter quantity of items:> ";
        cin >> quantitySold;
        // order of operations says * and divide first then add/sub unless forced by ( )
        float sub =  item_total * quantitySold;
        tax = sub * .07;

        cout << "sub total is:> " << sub;
        cout << "tax is:>  " << tax;

        total = sub + tax;

        cout << "Total amount due is:  ";
        cout << total  << "\n";

        system("pause");
        return 0;
}
```

Math operators

We have seen a few math operators, but good zombie hunters should be very familiar with all of them. So, with that introduction here they are:

* multiplication as in: x = c * .5;

+ addition as in: x = c + 5;

- subtraction as in: z = x - 1;

/ division as in: p = 4 / 2;

% modulus, or the remainder of integer division as in: b = 4 % 2;

To see one of these in action, key in and try the following:

```
//Modulus
#include <iostream>
 using namespace std;

int main()
{
        cout << "Modulus!" << endl;

        cout << "b = 4 % 2";

        int b;

        b = 4 % 2;

        cout << b;

        system("pause");
        return 0;
}
```

Challenge: Try the other math operators in a program of your choice.

Single selection structure, the *if* statement

You have been using all along one of the first basic control structures, the *sequence structure*. With this structure *the order of operations starts from the top, and moves along, line by line, until the last instruction is met.*

With a *single selection structure*, the *if*, a *statement is evaluated and executes only if it is true*, the statement(s) below it are executed, if not it is ignored and again the sequence structure moves forward. The very next line, beneath an if statement is the only one executed, unless a statement block is beneath it, enclosed in braces {}.

Statement blocks

You can group things to work together with statement blocks. Simply preface them with a left brace, and close with an ending brace and they will all execute as a unit.

To see the single selection structure in action, statement blocks, and how not to use them, examine the following code samples. In them you will find a peek ahead to some logical relational operators, the == which is the equality operator and tests to see if two items are equal, and the >= operator which checks to see if something is greater than or equal to a value. Try them out to see how they work.

```
//Single selection structure
#include <iostream>
 using namespace std;

int main()
{
        cout << "Single selection structure:" << endl;

        cout << "x=1";

        int x=1;

        if (x == 1)
           cout << "X must be 1!" << endl;

        system("pause");
        return 0;
}
```

In the next example you will see three if statements, all of which will be checked regardless if the first is true or not. In the next chapter we can improve on this logic. But for now consider the following:

```cpp
//Single selection structure not a good structure as all are checked
#include <iostream>
using namespace std;

int main()
{
        cout << "Single selection structure:" << endl;

        cout << "x=1";

        int x=1;

        if (x == 1)
                cout << "X must be 1!" << endl;

        if (x == 2)
                cout << "X must be 2!" << endl;

        if (x >= 100)
                cout << "X must be 100+!" << endl;

        system("pause");
        return 0;
}
```

Lastly let's look at a statement block, and then how not to write one!

The good:

```cpp
//Single selection structure with a statement block
#include <iostream>
 using namespace std;

int main()
{
        cout << "Single selection structure:" << endl;

        cout << "x=1";

        int x=1;
```

```
        if (x == 1)
        {
                cout << "X must be 1!" << endl;
                cout << "This fun!\n";
        }

        system("pause");

        return 0;
}
```

The bad and the ugly:

*If you have never heard of the Movie, "The Good, the Bad, and the Ugly"….use the Internet to expand your knowledge, every needs to know who Clint Eastwood is!

```
//Single selection structure wrong way!
#include <iostream>
 using namespace std;

int main()
{
        cout << "Single selection structure:" << endl;

        cout << "x=3";

        int x=3;

        if (x == 1)
                cout << "X must be 1!" << endl; // only if x == 1
                cout << "This fun!\n"; // executes everytime!!!!

        system("pause");
        return 0;
}
```

Note the *x* is 3, but the "This is fun!" always prints since it is not associated with the if (note no braces.

Getting user input with *cin*

So, you have seen that *cout* from the *iostream* library is used for console output. The *cin* keyword can be used to get user input from the keyboard. Basically you change the direction of the indirection operators << and >> to "point" to where you want the action to happen. E.g. Point the string data to the console as in: *cout* << *"Hello World"*   or for a variable value1 input from the user by the keyboard: *cin* >> *value1*   Examine the next bit of code to see it in action.

```cpp
// Performs basic operations on user inputted numbers
#include <iostream>
using namespace std;

// Start the program
int main()
{
        // Variable declarations
        int n1 = 0;              // User input 1
        int n2 = 0;              // User input 2
        int sum = 0;             // Sum of n1 and n2
        int diff = 0;            // Difference of n1 and n2
        int prod = 0;            // Product of n1 and n2
        int quot = 0;            // Quotient of n1 and n2

        // Give instructions to User and obtain their numbers
        cout << "Please enter two numbers to perform math operations on: \n";
        cin >> n1 >> n2;

        // Perform operations on the numbers
        sum = n1 + n2;
        diff = n1 - n2;
        prod = n1 * n2;
        quot = n1 / n2;
        // Display results
        cout << "The sum of your two numbers: " << sum << endl;
        cout << "The difference of your two numbers: " << diff << "\n";
        cout << "The product of your two numbers: " << prod << endl;
        cout << "The quotient is: " << quot << endl;
        // Keep command prompt up and Error check
        system("pause");
        return 0;
}       // End the program
// loss of precision means you have an int and need a float or something.
//warnings okay, halt bad.
```

That was good information we covered. Jot a few notes down and extend your learning to further your understanding.

Notes to remember

Learning extension

1. Create an application which asks for quantity and price of an item and gives the total price, integer variable are fine.

2. Using the application from problem 1, allow the program to check for 0 or negative values and allow the user to reenter a positive quantity.

3. Create an application which asks for three integer variables from the user and averages them.

4. Create an application which asks for three integer variables from the user and adds them.

5. Get two numbers from the user and see if the first is a multiple of the second.

6. Obtain two numbers from the user and display which is the lowest.

7. Obtain two numbers from the user and display which is the highest.

8. Create an application which gets price, quantity, and computes a sub total and total with .07% tax. Show all values to the user. Use floating point variables.

9. To problem 8 add in a check for 0 (zero) or negative quantity and allow the user to reenter a correct value if needed.

10. To problem 8 add in a check for 0 or negative price and allow the user to reenter a correct value if needed. Also add in a discount of 10% if the cost is over $100.

11. Odd or even. Create a program which checks if a number is odd or even, use modulus.

12. Heads or tails. Create a program which shows "Heads" or "Tails" if a number input by the user is odd or even.

Chapter 2

Relational and Equality Operators, Selection Structures, and Constants

The first chapter we covered a lot of good material, some of which was a peek ahead to things we will discuss in this chapter. You learned about the single selection structure, the *if* statement. Remember that the *if* statement looks for truth, and executes what is associated with it, and skips it if it is not true. Also recall that any statement on the very next line under an *if*, is associated with it. If more than one line, they must be surrounded in { } braces or you will not have a statement block for multiple lines or commands associated with the *if* statement. The end effect could be that your statements are indented under the *if*, and look quite reasonable, but yet only the first line under the *if* is associated with it unless you use { } braces to force a statement block.

Relational and equality logical operators

Now let's add a bit more on logical operators, that only seems logical right Mr. Spock? Consider the following table:

Operators

> Greater than

< Less than

>= Greater than/equal to

<= Less than/equal to

== Is the left side equal to the right side?

!= Is the left side not equal to the right side?

Now, following the same logic as the if statement, these operators are asking a question, and trying to determine truth or falsity, no in-between! E.g. "is it true X is greater than Y"? Even if they are the same, it is false, or if X is greater, it is true, etc.

Try the following to see these operators in action. Change the primary value to get different results.

```cpp
//relational and equality operators
#include <iostream>
 using namespace std;

int main()
{
        cout << "Logical comparison" << endl;

        cout << "The value we are comparing is x=3";

        int x=5;

        if (x < 1)
                cout << "x is less than 1\n";

        if (x <= 1)
                cout << "x is less than or equal to 1\n";

        if (x > 1)
                cout << "x is less than 1\n";

        if (x >= 1)
                cout << "x is greater than or equal to 1\n";

        if (x == 1)
                cout << "x is equal to 1\n";

        if (x != 1)
                cout << "x is not equal to 1\n";

        system("pause");
        return 0;
}
```

*Note that in the aforementioned example, each if executes a check, so in some respects it is not efficient if there was only one situation that would be true. If multiple situations might be true, then it is fine.

Big mistake!

Don't make the mistake of using a single equals sign when you want an equality double equals sign. Consider the following code which will always be true:

> x = 3 // assignment

> if (x = 1) // a single equals sign is assignment, setting x = to 1 even though it is within an *if*!

Problem! You can have if (x = 1) in some languages, such as VB.NET and it will perform an equality check, but C++ will note base its usage on context but will do exactly what you tell it,

regardless if this is what you want or not. So, make sure you use = = (two) equal signs for equality and only one for assignment!

Logical OR and logical AND

The OR operator, represented by the || (double pipes) is used to check if one or both sides of an evaluative condition is true.

Consider the following:

if ((x>1) || (x==7))

> **{do something....}**

With the aforementioned code snip, if either or both are true the whole *if* is true and executes.

The AND is represented by the **&&** signs. Consider:

if ((x > 1) && (y < 3))

> **{do something....}**

In this example both sides of the AND must be true for the *if* to execute. Try the following to see how they work.

```
//AND and OR
#include <iostream>
 using namespace std;

int main()
{
        cout << "AND and OR" << endl;

        int x=5;
        int y = 1;
```

28

```cpp
if ((x > 1) && (y==1)) // both sides must be true with AND
        cout << "x is greater than 1 and y is equal to 1\n";

if ((x >= 1) || (y > 100)) // one or both sides must be true with OR
        cout << "x is greater than or equal to 1 or y is greater than 100\n";

        system("pause");

return 0;
}
```

Short circuit evaluation

Short circuit evaluation states that if the statement cannot be true, due the first part, the second part will not be evaluated and of course the reverse is true since if the first part is true, the second part is not evaluated. Consider the following:

```cpp
//Sample short-circuit evaluation
#include <iostream>
using namespace std;

int main()
{
        int x = 1;
        int y = 2;

        if ((y == 2) || (x = 3))
        {
        cout << "y = " << y << " as it should" << endl;
        cout << "x still equals 1   >>>> " << x << " second part of the if did not execute" <<
endl;
        cout << "Logical OR wants one or both sides true. The first side is, so it does not set
x=3!" << endl;
        }

        cout <<
"=================================================================" << endl;
        cout << "An assignment statement is always true, note what happens next." << endl;

        if ((x = 3) || (y = 1000))
        {
        cout << "x is:  " << x << " now 3 since we set it to 3 in the IF!!!!" << endl;
        cout << "y is still 2! " << y << " and not 1000" << endl;
        }
```

29

```
        system("pause");

        return 0;
}
```

Note that in the second IF x is set to 3, and y is not set to 1000 since the short circuit found truth in the first part of the OR.

Yet more on IF statements, the ternary IF/ELSE operator

You can create simple one-line if statements to streamline your code with this operator.

The format is: *result = (x > 5) ? 1 : 0;*   where result might be an int variable and if x is greater than 5, result has a value of 1 stored in it, versus if it is less than 5 a 0 is stored. As you can see if it was a multiple-line if, this would not work. There are three operands in use which is why it is called the ternary operator.

Without using the ternary operator:

```
#include <iostream>  // without the ternary if
using namespace std;

int main()
{
        int result = 0;
        int x = 0;

        cout << "Enter a number: ";
        cin >> x;

        if(x > 5)
                result = 1;
        else
                result = 0;

        cout << "The result was:  " << result;

        system("pause");

        return 0;
}
```

Note how much more concise the code is! Again, though this is good for "one liners" only such as "a duck walks into a bar and orders a beer and a sandwich...."

```cpp
#include <iostream>  // with ternary if
using namespace std;

int main()
{
        int x = 0;

        cout << "Enter a number: ";
        cin >> x;

        int result = (x > 5) ? 1 : 0;

        cout << "The result was:  " << result;

        system("pause");

        return 0;
}
```

Boolean operators

These operators work on a bit by binary bit comparison, as opposed to the logical operators. In your programming efforts you may find them to give about the same results, but they are different.

Bitwise OR

This is represented by a single | only and works on a bit-bit comparison, but works similar to a logical OR.

Bitwise AND

This is represented by a single & and work in a similar fashion, but on a bit-by-bit comparison level. Both sides will be evaluated with this.

Complement ~

The tilde ~ will flip every bit, so **on** becomes **off** for each position. It is also known as the *complement* operator.

XOR

The ^ or caret operator is the XOR operator which is the **binary exclusive OR**. It will find truth only if one side is true and not both. Consider:

if ((x ==1) ^ (y < 2))

{do something....}

In the following, both sides are true, so the whole statement is false.

```
//Sample exclusive OR
#include <iostream>
using namespace std;

int main()
{
        int x = 1;
        int y = 2;

        if ((y == 2) ^ (x == 1))
                cout << "Do ot show this but show the else since it is false";

        else
        {
                cout << "y = " << y << " x = " << x << endl;
                cout << "y true and x true, but for XOR only one can be true" << endl;
                cout << "so the entire statement is false" << endl;
        }

        system("pause");

        return 0;
}
```

An example of the & operator. Note in the example that y does not equal 21, yet the second part is still evaluated, and there is no way the entire statement could be true. No short circuit evaluation takes place. It is as sad as 40 zombies and only having a 30 round magazine!!!

```
#include <iostream>
using namespace std;

int main()
{
        int x = 1;
        int y = 3;
```

```
if ((y == 21) & (x = 100))
        cout << "first is assignment, which is true" << endl;

cout << x;

system("pause");

return 0;
}
```

Dual selection structures with IF and ELSE

You learned about single selection structures with the IF statement, and have seen a peek ahead to the else, but let's formalize how it works. This is a structure which checks for truth with the IF and if it is not true, the ELSE executes.

```
// simple overview of dual selection structure with if /else
#include <iostream>
using namespace std;
int main()
{
        cout << "Example of simple if dual selection structure";
        int number = 0;
        cout << "Enter a positive value or a neg. value: ";
        cin >> number;
        if (number > 0)
                cout << "Postive value was: " << number << endl;
        else   // note! no evaluative condition such as else (number <= 0)
                cout << "\nNot a positive value"  <<endl;

        system("pause");

        return 0;
}
```

So, if you have more than three things to compare, a multiple section structure, such as the IF, ELSE IF, ELSE might be in order.

33

Multiple selection structures with If, Elseif, Elseif, Else

If you have more than two possible choices, you will want a form of multiple selection structure. Try out the code below then read on.

```cpp
// simple overview of multiple if else if else selection structure
#include <iostream>
using namespace std;

int main()
{
        cout << "Example of simple if dual selection structure";
        int number = 0;
        cout << "Enter a positive value or a neg. value: ";
        cin >> number;
        if (number > 0)
                cout << "Postive value was: " << number << endl;
        else if (number == 0)
                cout << "Value is zero" << endl;
        else
                cout << "\nNot a positive value"  <<endl;

        system("pause");

        return 0;
}
```

With an if/elseif/else structure, it is evaluated from the top down (sequential execution) until it finds truth, then it stops. If you need to evaluate all of the conditions, use multiple if statements. However, note that this will check all of them and not stop after it finds truth. Think of it as if you assumed all were infected zombies, which might not be the case.

Multiple selection structures with *Switch* statements

So, in the previous section you learned a bit about how to use selection structures. Sometimes you may find that for simple data, such as when sorting an *int* or *char* a *switch* is a cleaner solution. *Switch* statements are also found in other languages, such as JAVA with the same name, and in VB.NET as *Case Select* statements. Regardless of the name, a *switch* statement will look for truth sequentially down the structure, but will not stop executing once if finds truth and enters the structure until it encounters either the end or a break keyword. This can offer

34

some interesting help, programmatically, if used correctly. *Switch* statements do not offer the flexibility though if an *if/elseif/else* structure however.

Key things to note about a switch are that it will accept simple data, whole numbers and not fractional values nor strings. Also note that you want a break after each section otherwise it will not stop, but will "jump in" where if finds truth and continue until the end. Provide a default case at the end "just in case" for input errors (assuming valid input, this is not for input validation but to allow for a case not in the list. Lastly, note there is no break after default since this you are already at the end of the structure. Consider the following.

```cpp
// selection structures with switch and integer data
#include <iostream>
using namespace std;

int main()
{
        int n = 0;
        cout << "Enter a number between 1 and 5: ";
        cin >> n;

        switch (n)
        {
        case 1:
                cout << "you entered a 1!" << endl;
                break;
        case 2:
                cout << "you entered a 2!" << endl;
                break;
        case 3:
        case 4:
                cout << "you entered a 3 or 4" << endl;
                break;
        case 5:
                cout << "you entered a 5!" << endl;
                break;
        default:
                cout << "Not 1 through 5 eh?" << endl;
        }
        system("pause");
        return 0;
}
```

Now let's try it with *char* character data.

```cpp
// selection structures with switch and char data
#include <iostream>
using namespace std;

int main()
{
    char n = ' ';
    cout << "Enter a letter A - D:  ";
    cin >> n;

    switch (n) // note capitals versus lower case makes a difference!
    {
    case 'A':
        cout << "you entered a A!" << endl;
        break;
    case 'B':
        cout << "you entered a B!" << endl;
        break;
    case 'C':
        cout << "you entered a C" << endl;
        break;
    case 'D':
        cout << "you entered a D!" << endl;
        break;
    default:
        cout << "Not a letter we asked for, so sorry!" << endl;
    }

    system("pause");

    return 0;
}
```

Key in the example below to see how it works.

```cpp
// Simple example of a Switch multiple selection structure
#include <iostream>
using namespace std;

int main()
{
    int zombies;

    cout << "Please input how many zombies there are between 1 and 5 and I will tell you how many bullets you will need" << endl;  // Make sure this is all on one line!
```

```
        cin >> zombies;

        switch (zombies)
        {
            case 1:
                cout << "You need at least one bullet." << endl;
                break;
            case 2:
                cout << "You need at least two bullets." << endl;
                break;
            case 3:
                cout << "You need at least three bullets." << endl;
                break;
            case 4:
                cout << "You need at least four bullets." << endl;
                break;
            case 5:
                cout << "You need at least five bullets.  I would get an extra five round
magazine just in case." << endl;   // Make sure this is all on one line!
                break;
            default:
                cout << "Run!!!" << endl;
        } // end of switch


        system("pause");

        return 0;
}
```

Now, remember that we said break is important to keep it from executing all statements after it finds a true condition. Change what you just wrote to have the program not perform as expected. Run it with a value of *1* to see this effect in action.

```
// Simple example of a Switch multiple selection structure
#include <iostream>
using namespace std;

int main()
{
        int zombies;

        cout << "Please input how many zombies there are between 1 and 5 and I will tell you
how many bullets you will need" << endl;  // Make sure this is all on one line!
        cin >> zombies;
```

```cpp
        switch (zombies)
        {
                case 1:
                        cout << "You need at least one bullet." << endl;
                        //break;
                case 2:
                        cout << "You need at least two bullets." << endl;
                        //break;
                case 3:
                        cout << "You need at least three bullets." << endl;
                        //break;
                case 4:
                        cout << "You need at least four bullets." << endl;
                        //break;
                case 5:
                        cout << "You need at least five bullets.  I would get an extra five
                                round magazine just in case." << endl;
                                        // Make sure the above cout is all on one line!
                        //break;
                default:
                        cout << "Run!!!" << endl;
        } // end of switch

        system("pause");
        return 0;
}
```

Notice that after commenting out the *break*, it found truth at case 1, entered the structure, and continued through all of them since there was no way to break out of the structure, even the default executed! Try the next example with character data.

```cpp
// Example of a Switch structure with char data
#include <iostream>
using namespace std;

int main()
{
        char letter;

        cout << "Please input a single letter 'A' or 'a' :  " << endl;
        cin >> letter;

        switch (letter)
```

```
        {
                case 'A':
                        cout << "'A' was input!" << endl;
                        break;
                case 'a':
                        cout << "Lower case 'a' was input!" << endl;
                        break;
                default:
                        cout << "No letter a or A input!" << endl;
        }

        system("pause");
        return 0;
}
```

It could be that you created some form of menu for your application where a letter section might be handy to use. Now, knowing what we learned about how the break caused the structure to stop, or if missing it just passes through to the next, let's make a menu program where the user can enter either an A or a and the same option will be chosen.

```
// Example of a Switch structure with char data
#include <iostream>
using namespace std;

int main()
{
        char letter;

        cout << "    Choose your zombie assault weapon." << endl;

        cout << "                       _____ " << endl;
        cout << "         |\_____ ^^^^^_____(_____\_____"<< endl;
        cout << "    HH======#H###############H####################" << endl;
        cout << "             ####""""""""""""`##(_))#H\"""""Y#######" << endl;
        cout << "             ####   \#H\    `Y###"<< endl;
        cout << "             ####   \#H\    `Y##" << endl;
        cout << "" << endl;
        cout << "If you want an AR15 5.56mm enter (A)" << endl;
        cout << "If you want a AK47 7.62mm enter (B)" << endl;
        cout << "If you want a CETME .308mm enter (C):  " << endl;
        cout <<
"=============================================================" <<
endl;
```

39

```cpp
        cin >> letter;

        switch (letter)
        {
            case 'A':
            case 'a':
                cout << "AR15 is a good choice, light and accurate." << endl;
                break;
            case 'B':
            case 'b':
                cout << "AK47, easy to get ammo for, large capacity magazines, and light
but not particularly accurate." << endl; // put this all on one line!
                break;
            case 'C':
            case 'c':
                cout << "Precursor to HK G3 and a large caliber rifle, great stopping
power but fewer rounds per magazine." << endl; // put this all on one line!
                cout << "Make your shots count." << endl;
                break;

            default:
                cout << "Better get tennis shoes and run away!" << endl;
        }

        system("pause");

        return 0;
}
```

Note that the ASCII (American Standard Code for Information Interchange) art graphic of an AR16 rifle can be left out. Regardless this is a great example of how the cascading effect of entering into a switch structure. Note that it enters and move forward whether a capital or lower case letter is entered. If you do try the ASCII art, adjust the spacing to get your rifle to display properly as monitor resolution will affect the end result. Try out yet another simple example of *switch* statements.

```cpp
//Another simple example of a switch multiple section structure
#include<iostream>
using namespace std;
int main()
{
        int value;
        cout << "Enter a number between 1 and 5: ";
        cin >> value;

        switch (value)
        {
        case 1:
                cout << "Must be a 1!\n";
                break; // break is important as with a switch it jumps in when truth
                        //is found...then continues down regardless
                        //until end or break is encountered.  So, not if a 3 or 4 is entered it
                        //cascades through both.
                        //Lastly a default case is a good idea but no need for break after //that
                        //since it is at the end already. Woot!
        case 2:  // Note statement blocks work fine!
        {
                cout << "Dude you entered a two, way kool bro!!!\n";
                break;
        }
        case 3:
        case 4:
                cout << "Wow, must be a 3 or 4!\n";
                break;
        default:
                cout << "Bummer, not 1 - 4, must be something else!!!\n";
        }

        system("pause");
        return 0;     }
```

Well that ends things for this chapter fellow zombie hunters. Use the skills and power you have just learned to complete the challenges and push your understanding.

Notes to remember

Learning extension

1. Write a program which uses an *and* (&&) operator to check for a user id # and pin number. If both match the user may enter, if not tell them they may not enter.

2. Write a program which uses an *and* (&&) operator to check for a user id # and pin number. If both match the user may enter, if not tell them which one is wrong. If both are wrong let them know as well.

3. Write a program which uses an *or* (||) operator to check for a user's age >= 21 or a 1 if current military. If either is true, allow the user to enter. If neither is true, tell them they are not allowed in.

4. Write a program which allows you to select a weapon from a list, such as 1, 2, 3 or A, B, C. It should have a menu, and when the weapon is selected a switch selection structure should find the item selected and give a bit more information on it for the user.

5. Write a program which uses a ternary if to give either a 10% or 25% discount for sales. If sales total is over $100 give a 10% discount. If over $500 give 25%. Ask for quantity and price to determine the total and show the final price, with discount to the user.

6. Create an application which uses an if/else if/ else to determine if a user has entered a 1, 2, or any other number.

7. Write an application which uses the complement operator. Display the original and new values.

8. Write an application which assigns a grade to students based on test scores. Use a switch statement to assign an A for 90+ to 100, B for 80+ to 90, C for 70 to 80, and Z for course repeat if lower than 70.

9. Provide grade input validation for problem 8.

10. Write a zombie weapon management program. You have three types of weapons, which take, 1, 3, or 10 round increments. Based on the type of weapon chosen by the user, ask for how many packages of ammo they need and display the final amount to them. E.g. a Havoc launcher would take single rounds, so if they wanted ammo it would be straight quantity. If a Glock 17 pistol, then 17 rounds per clip, so if they wanted two, they would have 34 rounds. Be as creative as you wish and provide ASCII art for weapons if you choose.

11. Write an order entry program for a fast food restaurant. Have at least five items. Show the items and cost. Ask the user for how many of each. Compute the final total, with .07% tax. Use a switch structure to sort.

12. For problem #11 add in a check for negative quantities and allow the user to reenter a proper quantity.

13. Write a food menu order system using a switch. When the order is completed compute .07% tax and display subtotal, tax, and total.

14. Write an inventory system for a hardware store with 5-10 items. Use If/elseif/else logic to compute totals for items desired, tax at .07%, and a total.

Chapter 3

Errors, Constant variables, and Formatting output

Errors -- Design time, runtime, and logic

Errors are a fact of life when it comes to computer programming. How you handle not having enough ammo during a zombie assault, or a major outbreak and surviving is how well you think things out and keep your cool. It is the same thing with computer programming, stay cool and take it line-by-line.

Basically you could get an error at *design time where it would not compile* (you typed something wrong perhaps. You are designing your code still, and it is not good enough to run yet. E.g. you left off a semi colon.

Or, you could get your program to compile and run, but *at some point while running it would crash, a **runtime error***. You assigned a variable that was too small to hold the data you assigned it.

Lastly you could get the program to run but it might not do exactly what you wanted, e.g. you typed an addition symbol when you meant to type a subtraction symbol, so *it ran but did not give the correct answer due to a **logic error***. E.g. instead of subtracting from a total balance it added to your balance.

Constant variables

A constant variable seems funny (name-wise) but basically it is a variable you set one time, and then does not change (stays constant) throughout the life of the program. In previous examples variable changed during runtime, or more.

Thus we could say that the data varied (and where the term variable probably came from). However, there may well be times that *you want to set a variable (or some structure) once at design time, and then not allow any changes to take place*, whether intentional or not. This protection from accidental modification can be very handy. Enter the *constant variable*.

As a matter of programming style convention, **constants are always in all capital letters**, as opposed to variables which might be snake case or camel case. Again, this convention is for code readability and has nothing to do with syntax interpretation by the compiler. To see this in action, examine the next program where the key word const is used to make value not changeable. When you make the change (one line) Microsoft's Intellisense detects that you cannot change a constant and gives and error where shown in comments. Other compilers might allow you to compile and run it, with an associated error at *run-time versus and error at design time* as this example shows.

```
// example of constant
#include <iostream>
using namespace std;

int main()
{
    const int VALUE = 0;  // keyword const declares a variable constant

        cout << "Please enter a number";

        cin >> VALUE; // will get error here!!!!

        if (VALUE > 0)
                cout << " value was greater than 0 " << value << endl;

        // endl is just like \n

        system("pause");

        return 0;
}
```

So this shows that if you try to change a constant, an error occurs. Next is a good example of a constant. In this example we want to make sure there is no accidental modification of tax_rate.

```
#include <iostream>  // How to use a constant
using namespace std;

int main()
{
    const float TAX_RATE = .07;  // keyword const declares a variable constant

        float sub_total;

        cout << "Please enter a sub total: ";

        cin >> sub_total;
```

```
cout << " tax amount on sub total is:  " << sub_total * TAX_RATE << endl;

system("pause");

return 0;
}
```

Pre-processor directives to create constants

Another way to create a constant is to establish pre-processor directives, which look similar to library includes like when you use *iostream*. Use **#define** *name value* to create a named constant, with a value which will allow you to reference the name, but the value will be substituted in place of it during compile time. This will allow your code to be a bit more readable, but again is just as good as the previous way to declare constants. Examine the following to see how it works.

```
#include <iostream>
using namespace std;
#define PI 3.1415  // define PI as constant

int main()
{
        double r;
        double c;
        cout << "Enter radius: ";
        cin >> r;
        c = 2 * PI * r;
        cout << "If the radis is: " << r << "a circle would be: " << c << endl;
        system("pause");
        return 0;
}
```

Text formatting

Next we will learn a bit about *printf*, which offers some powerful formatting capabilities when compared to *cout*.

Note in the example that there are variable place holders, noted with the % sign and a value marker (such as d for integer, s for string, f for floating point, etc). The big thing to note is that

46

if you have three variable place holders, you will have three variables, after the closing quote, separated by commas. Where you have a variable place holder, the variable will replace it in the output. Consider the following:

```
//Formatting printed output to the console
#include<iostream>
using namespace std;

int main()
{
        int n = 1;
        printf("The variable n is %d \n", n);

        printf("And strings are printed with percent s as in %s \n", "Fred");
        //Note we could have used a variable but hard coded the string

        system("pause");

        return 0;
}
```

Now, let's try a bit more advanced example.

```
//Formatting printed output to the console
#include<iostream>
using namespace std;

int main()
{
        int n1 = 1;
        double n2 = 1.5555;
        char mychar = 'A';  // note single quotes for character

        printf("The var n1 is %d and the var n2 is %.2f \n", n1, n2);

        printf("And strings are printed with percent s as in %s \n", "Fred");

        printf("Characters are percent c as with %c \n", mychar);

        system("pause");

        return 0;
}
```

Note that %.2f will format for two decimal places of precision, good for dollar amounts. Try it with one or three places of precision to see how it works. You would use **%.1f** instead of what you tried above.

Escape codes for formatting

In previous examples you have seen how the **\n** command works the same as and **endl**. Other escape codes you find handy are:

\n -- add a hard return.

\r -- same as new line (hard return) above but sometimes useful if you are sending a job to the printer and not the screen. \f will have about the same effect. Most good zombie hunters use \n.

\t -- a tab. If you had three as in: \t\t\t it would tab 15 spaces, or five each tab.

\b -- backspace.

\a -- sounds the default system bell. This can be fun and annoying at the same time when performed often!

\' -- single quote.

\" -- show a double quote.

\? -- a question mark.

\\ -- print a backslash.

Try the example out to see some of them in action.

```
//Formatting with escape codes
//this would work with printf the same as shown with cout
#include<iostream>
using namespace std;

int main()
{
        cout << "ab\tcdefg\r";

        cout << "abcd\a\a\a\n";

        cout << "\ta \bbcd\n"; //there are two spaces but \b removes one

        cout << "\' \? \\ \? \n";
```

48

```
        system("pause");

        return 0;
}
```

Using *setw, setprecision,* and *setfill*

The *iomanip* library will help you to format your output. *Setw* will set the width of where a variable appears. *Setfill* will specify a character to fill the spaces you are trying to pad, and *setprecision* will set a number of numeric placeholders you specify (e.g. if you wanted only three decimal places of precision). Consider the following:

```
//setfill setw and setprecision
#include<iostream>
#include<iomanip>
using namespace std;

int main()
{
        int x = 6;

        float y = 1.1234;

        cout << "hello" << setfill('x') << setw(10) << "Hello\n";  // print 5 then pad 5's
                //and Hello again

        cout << setfill(' ') << setw(15) << x  << endl; // note space to reset
        setfill to        //nothing (default)
                                // remove the setfill and note it will still be x

        cout << setprecision(3) << y << endl; // shows three places of precision

        system("pause");
        return 0;
}
```

The *setfill()* function specifies a value to pad when using the *setw()* function which specifies an amount of width you may wish between items.

```
//setfill and setw
#include<iostream>
#include<iomanip>
using namespace std;

int main()
{
cout << setw(10) <<setfill('x') << "hello" << setw(15)  << "more hello" << "yet more hello\n";

        system("pause");
        return 0;
}
```

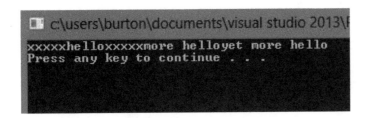

Figure 3.1 Output from setw().

As you can see, we wanted to output "hello" which is five spaces, but setw is set to 10, so there are five spaces of padding with 'x'. Then since setw is next set to 15, five are padded before the next string is displayed. Next let's try to aligning text and displaying a number in a different base, in this case hexadecimal base 16. Note *iomanip* is not used but is a feature of *iostream*. Of course there are other features as well you can easily research, so extend your knowledge after getting this to work and explore some others on your own.

```
#include<iostream>
using namespace std;

int main()
{
        int n = -77;
        cout.width(10);
        cout << internal << n << endl;  // do not move the sign
        cout.width(10);
        cout << left << n << "left" <<                 endl;
        cout.width(10);
        cout << right << n << "right" << endl;
        cout << hex << 14 << "   <- hex 14" << endl;  // 14 is e in base 16 hex numbering
```

```
        system("pause");

        return 0;
}
```

That is it for this chapter. Try your hand at the examples to practice and extend what you have learned.

Notes to remember

Learning extension

1. area is PI * Radius * Radius. Create a program which asks the user for radius and computes area as a floating point value. Designate PI with the const keyword to 3.14.

2. area is PI * Radius * Radius. Create a program which asks the user for radius and computes area as a floating point value. Designate PI as a constant via a pre processor directive to 3.14.

3. Invoice program. Create a program with asks for quantity and price for items. Declare TAX as a constant. Compute subtotal, total, and tax owed by the customer.

4. Card payments program. Create a program which sets credit card interest (such as .23%), asks user for amount owed on card, and computes a total which should be the amount + the amount * interest rate per month. Show the total, subtotal, and interest. Declare interest as a constant.

5. Use *setw* to create the output which follows:

			Values			
32	22	11	1	8	99	22
22	11	55	12	9	11	100
23	33	69	20	11	19	87

6. Using what you wrote for #3, include *setprecision* to two decimal places and *setfill* with a character of your choice around the final total.

7. If you knew you were "catching" errors there are the functions *cerr* and *clog* which work about the same as *cout*, but are for outputting errors and outputting to a log file or other device perhaps. Create a simple if/else program with uses *cout* to output an input value from the user if an even value or cerr/clog if an odd value. Note output will be the same. Use the Internet if curious on some of the history of these two functions.

8. MPG is computed as miles drive divided by gallons used. Set decimal precision to .1 and determine MPG based on user input of miles and gallons entered.

9. Velocity is computed as *velocity = distance / timetravelled* with the direction of East, West, etc. appended to it. Create a program with asks for distance, time travelled in hours or fractions of hours, and the direction. Output the results. A distance of 50 miles, in one hour eastward, would give a velocity of 50 MPH Eastward. Utilize setprecision, strings, and any formatting options to make the output attractive.

10. For problem 8 implement a form of error control with if statements to make sure values are positive. Allow the user a second chance to input values if incorrect.

11. For problem 9 implement a form of error control with if statements to make sure values are positive. Allow the user a second chance to input values if incorrect.

12. Allow for 10 grades to be input as whole numbers. Based on a 10 point scale, determine a grade for the student. Utilize if statements to output the students grade. Allow for input validation via if statements to make sure no negative or over 100 grades are entered.

Chapter 4

Looping structures, Functions, goto statements, and boolean operations

So, all good zombie hunters know the cycle of life (if undead) and that is that zombies eat the living and create more zombies. In this way zombies understand that there is a looping cycle to creating more zombies. For programmers we can get a bit more detailed and mimic this programmatically with two looping structures in C++ (the *while* loop and *for* loop) and actually a few variations on even how they are implemented. Interesting? You bet! Handy too.

There are several *looping structures* in C++ which you should be familiar with. Also known as *repetition structures*, they, just as you would imagine from the name, *repeat or iterate over a code segment until an event or certain count is obtained*. Variations on some of these looping structures include where this check for an event or amount is obtained (e.g. at the top of the loop or the bottom of the loop). Loop counters that work off a certain number of set repetitions at design time are referred to as *definite repetition* since you know at design time how many times the loop will run. Loop counters that work off an event are referred to as *indefinite repetition* and require a flag or sentinel value to be obtained before they become false and exit the loop. So, it should be understood that like an *if statement, loops are looking for truth to continue*.

Definite repetition with a while loop

Definite repetition is where you know at program design time how many iterations or cycles the loop will run. E.g. a loop will run ten times. If you did not enter your PIN properly three times, an ATM would lock your account. This is an example of definite repetition since you know at design time how many times an event will take place. Try an example of this with a *definite repetition while loop* structure.

```
// example of for loop with definite repetition
#include <iostream>
using namespace std;

int main()
{
        int counter =1;
        while (counter == 10)
```

```
        {
                cout << "Value of counter is:\a  " << counter << endl;
                counter++;
        }
        system("pause");
        return 0;
}
```

Indefinite repetition with a *while* loop

If you do not know how many times a loop will run at design time, then indefinite repetition is just the ticket. Just make sure you have a way to get out of the loop, or that you inform the user of how to get out of the loop if user control is in order. Consider as a first example the following:

```
// indefinite repetition with while
#include <iostream>
using namespace std;

int main()
{
        int counter=1;  // initial value for while

        int zombies=0;

        cout << "how many zombies are there to shoot?";

        cin >> zombies;

        while (counter < zombies)
        {
        cout << "Value of counter is:\t  " << counter << "bang! one zombie gone!\a" <endl;

        counter = counter + 1;  // take one away one zomie  e.g. decrement by 1

        }
        system("pause");

        return 0;
}
```

So in the previous example we only knew at run-time how many zombies there were. Read on to learn more.

Sentinel or flag values and indefinite repetition

```cpp
// indefinite repetition while and flag value
#include <iostream>
using namespace std;

int main()
{
        int counter=1;

        while (counter != 999)
        {
        cout << "Enter a number or enter 999 to exit " << endl;

        cin >> counter;
        }
        system("pause");
        return 0;
}
```

The previous example does nothing but take a value, and if it is 999 it exits, but it will run forever, or until 999 is entered so it shows indefinite repetition. Now that you have see how *while* loops work, let's try our hand with *for* loops. Next try another example.

```cpp
//Product total sales using switch statement and sentinel or flag value
//indefinite repetition example
#include<iostream>
using namespace std;

int main()
{
        float cost = 0;
        int quantity = 0;
        int item = 0;

        cout << "Select a product to purchase 1 - 5, or 6 to exit: ";
        cin >> item;

        while (item != 6)
        {
        switch (item)
                {
                case 1:
                        cout << "how many of item 1? ";
                        cin >> quantity;
```

```cpp
                cost += 2.98 * quantity;
                break;
        case 2:
                cout << "how many of item 2? ";
                cin >> quantity;
                cost += 4.50 * quantity;
                break;

        case 3:
                cout << "how many of item 3? ";
                cin >> quantity;
                cost += 9.98 * quantity;
                break;

        case 4:
                cout << "how many of item 4? ";
                cin >> quantity;
                cost += 6.87 * quantity;
                break;

        default:  // optional!!!!
                cout << "Should not see this!!";    }

        cout << "Select a product to purchase 1 - 5, or 6 to exit: ";
        cin >> item;

    }  // end while
    cout << "Total cost was: " << cost << endl;

    system("pause");
    return 0;        }
```

For loops

For loops work in the same way as a while but with a while you have the initialization value before the while, with a *for* statement it is neatly bundled in with the actual structure. The format is: initial value to start with, evaluative condition looking for truth, and the increment amount. Note that only the increment amount is not followed by a semi colon.

So as an example: *for (int start=1; start < 10; start++)* where you would have a loop which would execute 10 times, counting by one via the post increment operator ++. Try it with definite repetition as follows below.

Definite repetition with a *for* loop

```cpp
// example of for loop definite repetition
#include <iostream>
using namespace std;

int main()
{
        for (int counter = 1; counter < 10; counter++)
        {
                cout << "Value of counter is:\a  " << counter << endl;
        }

        system("pause");

        return 0;
}
```

With the previous example we saw how a *for* can be used for definite repetition. However it can be used for indefinite as well. Consider the following.

Indefinite repetition with a *for* loop

```cpp
// example of for loop indefinite repetition
#include <iostream>
using namespace std;

int main()
{
        int runTime;

        cout << "How many times to run loop?:  ";

        cin >> runTime;

        for (int counter = 1; counter <= runTime; counter++)
        {
                cout << "Value of counter is:\a  " << counter << endl;
        }

        system("pause");

        return 0;
}
```

Note that with a *while* loop, you need to initialize the *while* counter before you go into it, and it needs to be initialized such that the *while* will be true at least one time, and within the *while* the counter is incremented (or decremented) so that the *while* will eventually prove true...so that you can get out of the darned thing!

However, the *for* loop has all the initialization and amount to count up or down by, in the main body of the loop. Both work the same, so pick whichever fits your needs better. Now that you have seen some examples of repetition, definite and indefinite, it is time for a practical example that provides some value. In this next example, you will find the smallest number from a selection of values.

```cpp
//Find the smallest value
#include<iostream>
using namespace std;

int main()
{
        int count = 0;
        int current;
        int smallest = 0;

        cout << "Enter values to find the smallest, first will be number to examine (sep.
                by space): ";
        cin >> count;
        cin >> current;
        smallest = current;
        for (int numbers = 1; numbers < count; numbers++)
        {
                cin >> current;
                if (current < smallest)
                        smallest = current;
        }

        cout << "smallest was " << smallest << endl;

        system("pause");

        return 0;
}
```

Now let's average some values. Definite repetition but you could end it early (and would want to!) by entering 9999.

```cpp
//sub procedures and function
#include<iostream>
using namespace std;

int main()
{
        int repetitions = 0;
        int value = 0;
        int sum = 0;

        cout << "Please enter values to average, 9999 to exit: " << endl;

        for (int counter = 1; counter <= 9999; counter++)
        {

                cin >> value;
                if (value == 9999)
                        break;

                repetitions += 1;
                sum += value;
        }

        cout << "Average of the numbers is: " << (sum / repetitions) << endl;

        system("pause");

        return 0;
}
```

Do-While loops

Do-while loops work in a similar fashion to regular while and for loops, yet are different in that *they check for truth at the bottom of the loop structure and not the top*. So *they will run one time regardless of the truth or falsity of the evaluative condition*. Other than that they are the same. Use them when you need the loop to run one time regardless of the evaluation. As an example, a password checking program would always check at least one time for the user's password.

```cpp
//Simple example of a do-while loop
#include<iostream>
using namespace std;

int main()
{
        int runs;
        cout << "Enter a 5 please: ";
        cin >> runs;

        do
        {
          cout << "This is a loop that checks for truth at the bottom, so it will run
        regardless of truth or falsity one pass.\n";
        } while (runs == 3);  // to be true runs would need to be a 3 but it still ran
                                once with 5 note this is = = for equality!
        system("pause");
        return 0;
}
```

Next we will consider *functions*. *Functions* are reusable segments of code and are very important to have a good understanding of.

Functions

You might think of a function as a reusable piece of code. If there is a part of code you might wish to use more than once, then it might fit well as a function. The process of creating functions can also make your code more readable (easy to understand) and easier to debug. If they sound like a good thing...they are!

Conceptually , and this will change a bit between which book you are reading or who you are talking to, think about functions in terms of sub procedures and functions.

A **sub procedure**, for our definition, will be a reusable piece of code that does something, but that is all. A **function**, again by our definition, is a reusable piece of code that returns a value to the calling function. With a function you will have the **key word return** in it. Some books do not make a distinction of the two though, so don't get too hung up on it. Let's explain a bit by looking at two simple examples.

```cpp
//Simple sub procedure
#include<iostream>
using namespace std;

void show_me(int x)// function defined before used
{
        cout << "Value is:  " << x;
}

int main()
{
        int t = 4;

        show_me(t);

        system("pause");
        return 0;
}
```

This example did a few neat tricks. First a sub procedure (it just shows a variable) named *show_me* was declared, which happen to require a variable to be given to it (in this case *t*). It copies, **pass by value**, *t* into the *x* variable, and then displays it.

Important things to note are that *t is copied into x* with pass by value, so any changes to *t*, performed in the sub procedure when it is copied to *x*, would not be reflect back on *t*. Also, nothing is returned, as in a function which we will see an example of soon. Now, does a sub procedure, or function require a value to be given to it? Nope. Consider the following example.

```cpp
//Simple sub procedure with no arguements
#include<iostream>
using namespace std;

void show_hello()
        {
         cout << "Hello\n";
        }

int main()
{
        show_hello();

        system("pause");
        return 0;   }
```

Note it works the same as the example before it. Now, things will start to get a little crowded if we define several sub procedures before we start the main body of our code. Consider that the following works, but is a bit hard to read (which we can improve).

```cpp
//Simple sub proceduress...a bit messy up top!
#include<iostream>
using namespace std;

void show_1()
{
        cout << "Hello one!\n";
}
void show_2()
{  cout << "Hello two!\n";  }  // note it can all go on one line
void show_3()
{
        cout << "Hello three!\n";
}

int main()
{
        show_1();
        show_2();
        show_3();

        system("pause");
        return 0;
}
```

Note that if you had more than a *cout* in the sub procedure declarations, it would take up a page or more before you started the main function! Now let's consider a sub procedure that has some value.

```cpp
//Simple sub proceduress..check if patron is 21 or younger
#include<iostream>
using namespace std;

void check_age(int age)//age_reported is passed by value (copied) into age
{
        if (age > 20)
                cout << "You are allowed in!\n";
        else if (age == 20)
                cout << "You are almost there, one more birthday!\n";
```

```
        else
                cout << "You are too young.\n";
}

int main()
{
        cout << "Enter your age please:   \n";
        int age_reported;
        cin >> age_reported;
        check_age(age_reported);

        system("pause");
        return 0;
}
```

Now, this example was cool, but if you had more than three things in the *if* it could again get messy and hard to read. So, *function prototypes* to the rescue!!!!!

Function prototypes

Function prototypes are really neat in that you only *define the basics of the sub procedure at the top of your code, and at the end of the program main body code you specifically define how the function works*. So, the first is a prototype which is defined at the bottom. Consider a modification of the previous example to see it in action.

```
//Simple sub procedure with a function prototype
#include<iostream>
using namespace std;

void check_age(int);  // func prototype ...said it needs an int, define at the bottom

int main()
{
        cout << "Enter your age please:   \n";
        int age_reported;
        cin >> age_reported;
        check_age(age_reported);

        system("pause");
        return 0;
}

void check_age(int age)
```

```
{
        if (age > 20)
                cout << "You are allowed in!\n";
        else if (age == 20)
                cout << "You are almost there, one more birthday!\n";
        else
                cout << "You are too young.\n";
}
```

Neat eh? Try a few more on to see them in action.

```
//sub procedures and function
#include<iostream>
using namespace std;

void add_them(int);  // function prototype
int add_return(int);

int main()
{
        int n1 = 10;

        cout << "The number multiplied by 2 is: " << endl;

        add_them(n1);

        cout << add_return(n1)  << endl;

        system("pause");
        return 0;
}

int add_return(int value)
{
        return value + 1;  }

void add_them(int number) // function def.
{
        cout << number * 2;  }
```

In the next example, consider a program to summarize values, and a second version which is functionalized via sub procedure.

```cpp
#include<iostream> // non-sub procedure version
using namespace std;

int main()
{
        int count = 0;
        int value = 0;
        int sum = 0;

        cout << "Please enter how many values to sum: " << endl;

        cin >> count;

        for (int counter = 1; counter <= count; counter++)
        {
                cin >> value;
                sum += value;
        }

        cout << "sum of " << count << " values was: " << sum << endl;

        system("pause");

        return 0;
}
```

And now the sub procedure functionalized version.

```cpp
#include<iostream> // Sub procedure version
using namespace std;

void sum_them(int);

int main()
{
        int count = 0;

        cout << "Please enter how many values to sum: " << endl;

        cin >> count;

        sum_them(count);

        system("pause");

        return 0;
}
```

```cpp
void sum_them(int the_count)
{       int value = 0;
        int sum = 0;
        for (int counter = 1; counter <= the_count; counter++)
        {
                cout << "Enter value " << counter << endl;
                cin >> value;
                sum += value;           }

        cout << "sum of " << the_count << " values was: " << sum << endl;
}
```

Note that the main body of code is somewhat abstracted (a good thing) from the function, so it is a bit easier to read. This abstraction of implementation details is a term we will get back to in future chapters. Suffice to say it can make our code easier to read.

Simple example of a function (or sub procedure which returns a value)

Now we will create functions (or sub procedures which return a value). They work in the exact same fashion, but will have the *key* or *system reserved word* "**return**" and can only give back a single value, not multiple items. In this next example let's check for good even numbers or zombie odd numbers.

```cpp
#include<iostream> // function which returns a value if odd or even
using namespace std;

int show_it(int);

int main()
{
        int number = 0;
        cout << "Even numbers safe, odd numbers are zombie, enter a number: " << endl;
        cin >> number;
        int result = show_it(number);
        if (result == 0)
                cout << "safe even number!\n";
        else
                cout << "Zombie number..it is odd!!!\n";

        system("pause");
        return 0;
```

```
}

int show_it(int value)
{
        if (value % 2 == 0)
                return 0;     //it is even
        else
                return 1;  //it is odd
}
```

Next, let's look at a similar version with boolean values.

```
#include<iostream> // function which returns a value if odd or even
using namespace std;

bool show_it(int);
int main()
{
        int number = 0;
        cout << "Even numbers safe, odd numbers are zombie, enter a number: " << endl;
        cin >> number;
        int result = show_it(number);

        if (result)///true is implied
                cout << "Safe!";
        else
                cout << "Zombie";

        system("pause");
        return 0;
}

bool show_it(int value)
{
        if (value % 2 == 0)
                return 1;     //it is even
        else
                return 0;  //it is odd
}
```

Both of the aforementioned examples are a bit wordy and could be streamlined, but they do show how the process works. One shows an integer solution, the other a bool solution.


```
// Example of find the smallest value
```

```cpp
#include<iostream>
using namespace std;

int smallest;// note this is outside of main()

void smallest_test(int value1)
{
        if (value1 < smallest)
                smallest = value1;
}

int main()
{
        int runs = 0;

        int count = 1;
        int number;

        cout << "Please enter number of values then enter each value to find smallest: " << endl;
        cout << "Number of values to enter?:  ";
        cin >> runs;  // first number entered is loop controller
        cout << "Enter value:  ";
        cin >> smallest;  // assume second number is smallest so far

        while (count < runs)  // less than and not <= since first number is loop counter only
        {
                cout << "Enter next number : ";
                cin >> number;
                smallest_test(number);  // test the value in our function, swap if smallest

                count++;
        }
        cout << "Smallest is: " << smallest << endl;
        system("pause");
        return 0;
}
```

In the next example we will prove that the value passed to a function is in fact copied (pass by value).

```cpp
#include<iostream> // function which returns a value if odd or even
using namespace std;

void copy_it(int z)
```

```cpp
{
        int x = 0;

        z = x; //set z to 0

        cout << z << " is the value of variable copied to the sub procedure" << endl;
}

int main()
{
        int number = 7;
        copy_it(number);  // copy 7 to the sub

        cout << "Number is still:  " << number << " since it was a copy only that was
changed!\n";

        system("pause");

        return 0;
}
```

You can **return *strings*** as well, which is pretty neat. Consider the following:

```cpp
#include<iostream> // function which returns a string
#include<string>
using namespace std;

string show_and_return_it(void)
{
        return "I can return strings!!!  ";
}

int main()
{
        cout << show_and_return_it();

        system("pause");

        return 0;
}
```

We will work more with functions, sub procedures, etc. since there is much more to it, but this should get you started and have given you a foundation to build on. Try the examples at the end of the chapter to hone your skills.

Notes to remember

Learning extension

1. Create an ATM PIN checking program. It should only allow the user to enter an incorrect PIN three times before locking the account.

2. Change program 1 to clear all incorrect attempts before leaving/program end.

3. Streamline the following code to be more efficient, keeping the function though. Change anything you wish.

```cpp
#include<iostream> // function which returns a value if odd or even
using namespace std;

int show_it(int);

int main()
{
        int number = 0;
        cout << "Even numbers safe, odd numbers are zombie, enter a number: " << endl;
        cin >> number;
        int result = show_it(number);
        if (result == 0)
                cout << "safe even number!\n";
        else
                cout << "Zombie number..it is odd!!!\n";

system("pause");

        return 0;
}

int show_it(int value)
{
        if (value % 2 == 0)
                return 0;    //it is even
        else
                return 1;  //it is odd
}
```

4. Given that a user enters 5 – 10 values (odd and even), determine which are odd or even using modulus, and output the sum of all of the odd values and all of the even values. You determine the number of values.

5. Create a program which allows users to enter student grades (whole numbers) until the user enters a -1. Average the numbers entered but do not include -1 in the average (but you knew that already!).

6. Using this code, create a functionalized version.

```
//sub procedures and function

#include<iostream>
using namespace std;

int main()
{
        int repetitions = 0;
        int value = 0;
        int sum = 0;
        cout << "Please enter values to average, 9999 to exit: " << endl;

        for (int counter = 1; counter <= 9999; counter++)
        {

                cin >> value;
                if (value == 9999)
                        break;

                repetitions += 1;
                sum += value;
        }

        cout << "Average of the numbers is: " << (sum / repetitions) << endl;

        system("pause");
        return 0;
}
```

7. Convert to have function prototype.

```
 // Example of find the smallest value
#include<iostream>
using namespace std;

int smallest;// note this is outside of main()
```

72

```cpp
void smallest_test(int value1)
{
        if (value1 < smallest)
                smallest = value1;
}

int main()
{
        int runs = 0;

        int count = 1;
        int number;

        cout << "Please enter number of values then enter each value to find smallest: " << endl;
        cout << "Number of values to enter?:  ";
        cin >> runs;  // first number entered is loop controller
        cout << "Enter value:  ";
        cin >> smallest;  // assume second number is smallest so far

        while (count < runs)  // less than and not <= since first number is loop counter only

        {
                cout << "Enter next number : ";
                cin >> number;
                smallest_test(number);  // test the value in our function, swap if smallest

                count++;
        }
        cout << "Smallest is: " << smallest << endl;
        system("pause");
        return 0;
}
```

8. Create a tax computing program, with a function, which proves that the tax amount is pass-by-value.

9. Create a program, with functions, which returns first and last names to an output statement.

10. Create a MPG program with a function to complete the computation.

11. Create an application which would compute calories burned based on various exercises and duration. Use functions as appropriate.

Chapter 5

Multiple parameter sub procedures, Overloaded functions, Pass by Reference, GOTO statements

Up to now we have had sub procedures and functions which took at most one argument. However, you certainly could require more. Note how this works in the next simple example of multiple parameters and sub procedures.

```cpp
#include<iostream> // sub procedure with two parameters
using namespace std;

void take_two(int, int);

int main()
{
        take_two(3, 8);

        system("pause");

        return 0;
}

void take_two(int a, int b)
{
        cout << "First number was:  " << a << endl;
        cout << "Second number was:  " << b << endl;
}
```

Overloaded functions

Of course this would work if you had prototypes or not. One of the neat aspects of this however is that you can *overload* functions giving them only a different signature to make them different, yet they have the same name. Think of a *signature as a different number or type of arguments* for our purposes here.

Consider the next example, yet note the sub procedures have the same name, and the one that is called is automatically (automagically????? Ha!) selected based on the signature.

```cpp
#include<iostream> // Overloaded sub procedures
using namespace std;

void take_two(int, int);

void take_two(double, double);

void take_two(int, int, int);

int main()
{
        take_two(1, 2);
        take_two(1.5, 2.3);
        take_two(100, 200, 300);

        system("pause");
        return 0;
}

void take_two(int a, int b)
{
        cout << "First int was:  " << a << endl;
        cout << "Second int was:  " << b << endl;
}
void take_two(double a, double b)
{
        cout << "First double was:  " << a << endl;
        cout << "Second double was:  " << b << endl;
}
void take_two(int a, int b, int c)
{
        cout << "First int of three was:  " << a << endl;
        cout << "Second int of three was:  " << b << endl;
        cout << "Third and final int was:  " << c << endl;
}
```

So, depending on what you give it (int versus double) and how many (two or three) determines which is used...again automatically via overloaded functions.

Default arguments

In the next example let's make a change and have one sub procedure, but we will assign a default value if the program does not give the sub values that it requires. In the next example, two are required and if not given it will assign a 1 and 3 respectively.

```cpp
#include<iostream> // default values
using namespace std;

void a_and_b(int n1 = 1, int n2 = 3)
{
        cout << "First int was:  " << n1 << endl;
        cout << "Second int was:  " << n2 << endl;
}

int main()
{
        a_and_b();
        cout << "both defaults used\n\n";

        a_and_b(8);
        cout << "only the second used since we gave it the first\n\n";
        a_and_b(2, 6);

        cout << "only new values are used, both default ignored\n";

        system("pause");
        return 0;
}
```

In the next example let's prove out how *Pass by value* works. Remember *Pass by value is a copy of the variable*.

```cpp
#include<iostream> // Pass by value
using namespace std;

int copy_only(int n1)
{       n1 = n1 + 2;
        return n1;  }

int main()
{
        cout << "Pass by value. No zombies harmed in the filming of this example!\n\n";
        int number = 1;

        cout << "New Value for copy of n1 is:  " << copy_only(number); // Number to n1
        cout << endl << "Number though is still:  " << number << endl;

        system("pause");
        return 0;
}
```

Pass by Reference

There are two ways to "hand off" so to speak, variables -- *pass by value* and *pass by reference*. Pass by value is, as we have seen, where a variable is copied to a sub procedure or function. *Pass by reference is where the location in memory is given to the sub procedure, so basically you are giving the sub procedure directions on where the original value is, and not a copy of it.* This is important since you might change the original value whereas with pass by value you would only be working on a copy.

The syntax for *Pass by reference* is as easy as a zombie head shot with a scope -- pretty easy. You will use the & sign before the variable to note that it points to where the variable is in memory, and is not a copy of the variable passed to it.

```cpp
#include<iostream> // Pass by reference only
using namespace std;

void add_it(int &x)
{       x = x + 1;   }

int main()
{
        int number = 5;
        cout << number << endl; // number is 5

        add_it(number); // we added 1 to the orig variable

        cout << number << endl; // number is 6, added 1!!!!

        system("pause");

        return 0;
}
```

So, in the previous example we printed out *number*, which was 5. Next *number* was accessed from the *add_it()* function and one was added to it. Next *number* was printed again, but it had been updated via the sub procedure by one, so six was displayed. While only one variable was "pointed to" in this example, you certainly could have several variables, and you could mix some passed by reference and some passed by value in the same sub procedure.

```cpp
#include<iostream> // Pass by value and pass by reference
using namespace std;

void add_it(int &x) // add to original variable
{        x = x + 1;   }
void add_it_local(int x) // add to copy only
{        x = x + 1;   }

int main()
{
        int number = 5;
        int number_local=5;
        cout << number << endl; // number is 5
        cout << number_local << endl;  //number is 5
        add_it(number); // we added 1 to the orig variable
        add_it_local(number_local);  //add to x in function only!
        cout << number << " via pass by ref one added to number"  << endl;
        cout << number_local << "via pass by value so original value kept!" << endl;

        system("pause");
        return 0;
}
```

Static local variables and scoping rules

So, think of *scoping* as *where you can get to a variable*. It is interesting to note that you can have variables with the same name, yet they are different areas of storage in memory and can be accessed based on where you are referencing them in a program. For example you can have a variable named *x* in *int main()* and you can have one named *x* in a function, and in fact you could have others as well with the same name, yet all are different variables in memory, and might be different data types or the same. Where you are when you reference them determines which you will access. E.g. if you are in *int main()* and reference *x*, then you will use that one and not one in a function. Yet if you were in the function, the *x* in *int main()* would be masked or hidden until you left the function. Whew! That was a lot, but we will see how it works in a minute.

Static local variables are *local variables that are not destroyed (automatically) when you leave the local function scope*. Normally if you create a variable in a sub procedure, it is destroyed when you leave. However, there may be times when you want the variable to keep its value. Perhaps you have an event counter that is contained in the sub procedure. You could make the variable static so that you knew how many times the sub procedure was called. Consider the code that follows to see scoping rules and static local variables in action.

```
//Masking variables with the same name and static local variables
#include<iostream>
using namespace std;

int x = 5;

void inner_x();
void use_outer();
void static_local_x();

int main()
{
        int x = 1;

        cout << x << " x in int main" << endl;

        inner_x(); // print x in sub procedure

        static_local_x();  // prints x with one added

        use_outer(); // print x before int main

        static_local_x(); // last value of static x plus one more

        use_outer(); // print x before int main again

        system("pause");

}
void inner_x()
{
        int x = 7;
        cout << x << " x in sub" << endl;
}

void use_outer()
{
        cout << x << " Outer x" << endl;  // x about int main
}

void static_local_x()
{
```

```cpp
        static int x = 1;
        x++;
        cout << x << " static x holds previous value" << endl;
}
```

Let's look at another example to further add to our understanding of this important concept.

```cpp
//Pass by value and pass by reference
#include<iostream>
using namespace std;

void pass_by_value(int);
void pass_by_ref(int &);

int main()
{
        int x = 1;
        int z = 3;
        cout << x << " x before pass value sub" << endl;

        pass_by_value(x);

        cout << x << " x after pass value sub..note did not hold value" << endl;

        cout << z << " z before pass ref not in sub" << endl;

        pass_by_ref(z);

        cout << z << " z after pass ref not in sub" << endl;

        system("pause");

        return 0;
}
void pass_by_value(int number)
{
        cout << number << " x in pass value" << endl;
        number++;
        cout << number << " x in pass value after increment" << endl;
}
void pass_by_ref(int &value)
{
        cout << value << " z in pass ref" << endl;
        value++;
        cout << value << " z in pass ref after increment" << endl;
}
```

Next we will examine what to do when you have a horde of zombies attacking. One is easy enough to handle, but with many, things get a little different.

Functions with Multiple Arguments and Default values

We have had functions that take only one argument. You can however have different arguments, and in fact, different types of arguments. This last part opens up a neat feature in programming where the signature (or types of data) determine which function is called, even if the function names are the same! Think of it as having a drum magazine on your zombie rifle as opposed to a five round magazine, not good during a zombie horde attack! Consider the following example with multiple arguments in the function.

```cpp
//Multiple arguments
#include<iostream>
using namespace std;

void takes_two(int, int);
int three_is_fun(int, char, int);

int main()
{
        char letter = "Z";
        int number = 8;
        int value = 4;

        takes_two(number, value);

        int result = three_is_fun(2, letter, 2);

        cout << result << " is the two parameters added together!" << endl;

        system("pause");

        return 0; // end of the program
}
void takes_two(int n1, int n2)
{
        cout << n1 << " times " << n2 << = << n1 * n2  << endl;
}
```

```
void three_is_fun(int n1, char let, int n2)
{
        cout << let << " is the letter";
        return n2 + n2;
}
```

Operator overloading

You just saw a function prototype and definition with two ints and a character. For the next

segment, consider where we have functions with the same name, but different signatures (e.g. the

argument types are different, which is **operator overloading**.

```
//Functions with same name but different signatures
#include<iostream>
using namespace std;

void simple(int);
void simple(int, int);
int simple(int, int, float);

int main()
{
        int num1 = 1;
        int num2 = 2;
        float num3 = 3.144;

        float result = simple(num1, num2, num3);

        cout << result << " is the float!" << endl;

        system("pause");

        return 0; // end of the program
}
void simple(int n1)
{
        cout << n1 << " is the value of num1 " << endl;
}
void simple(int n1, int n2)
{
        cout << n1 * n2 << " is the value of num1 times num2 " << endl;
}
int simple(int n1, int n2, float f3)
{
```

```
        cout << n1 << " is num1 " << n2 << " is num2 " << endl;
        return f3;
}
```

From the preceding example you can see that the functions all have the *same name, yet there are different signatures.* For example, one has a return value whereas the other two do not, yet they take a differing number of arguments. So, the signature decides which is called.

Goto statements

The Boehm and Jacopini theorem states that with structured programming *you will only need three structures.* Dijkstra proposed based on their work three structures, sequence (also known as concatenation but not in the terms of joining string data), selection, repetition, and optionally stop or halt which may or may not be supported by the language. We have discussed this before but again sequence is the flow of a program or structure from the beginning to the end, selection could be exemplified by an *if* statement, etc., and repetition would be looping structures such as *while* and *for* loops.

As such, *goto* statements do not fit into one of these three areas and predate the aforementioned researchers work. They do not allow jumps or program control flow to be as easily traceable when compared to the three structures listed. So, the *goto* works, but it is tougher to "follow" when you are examining the logical flow of a program. That being said it is a valid structure in C++ though, and any good zombie hunter will want to at least know how it works, but be careful and limit your use of this tool though! Examine the following code which implements a *goto.*

```
// a goto statement
#include <iostream>
using namespace std;

int main()
{
        int number = 5;

        for (int count = 1; count < number; count++)
        {
                cout << count << endl;

                if (count == 3)
```

```
                    goto exit_me;
        }

exit_me:
        cout << "leaving at three!\n";
        system("pause");
}
```

The previous example is very simple, but yet it demonstrates a **goto** statement. If the counter is equal to three, then it jumps to the *exit_me* **goto** statement, which displays a message and holds the terminal window open until the user (on a DOS system) presses a key. Try the problems at the end of the chapter to reinforce what you have learned.

Notes to remember

Learning extension

1) Create an application which computes tax. Use two overloaded functions, one which accepts an int, and one a float.

2) Create an application which determines clip capacity for rifles based on a numeric value. E.g. a 1 is and AR-15, 2 is a Glock, etc. You chose style and capacity. If two values are given, say an int and a character, then a primitive zombie killing weapon is selected. E.g. a 1 and a c for crossbow. Feel free to include switch statements, if statements, etc. Bonus for ASCII art!

2) Be creative and write an application which uses overloaded operators.

3) Create a simple selection program, using an if/else.

4) Create the same program you wrote in #3 above, but use goto statement(s).

5) Create a program with a sub procedure which uses only variable pass by value and one variable pass by reference. Prove that both work each way. The sub procedure should have both types in it.

6) Create a program with an if statement which calls a function. Create a second version where goto statements are used instead.

7) List at least one advantage and one disadvantage to using a GOTO statement.

8) Create an application with a sub procedure which has a default value, such as tax_rate=.07 unless the user passes a different value.

9) Write a math learning assistant program using function prototypes and function definitions. Allow for the user to select A for addition, S for subtraction, etc. You should have a function for each.

10) Create an application which computes monthly interest earned on money in a bank. Allow the user to enter the amount, interest amount, and months interest use be tabulated. Use set precision for two decimal places of precision.

11) Research BMI and write a functionalized program which computes BMI.

12) Adapt problem #11 to suggest methods to gain or lose weight if they are not in the acceptable range. Bonus for ASCII art.

Chapter 6
Arrays, Vectors, Tuples, and Lists

You have learned about different variable data types (such as integers, floating point values, etc.) As you have probably surmised, they are stored in memory that the OS has determined is free for use. That being said they are not necessarily stored in some sequential order in memory as far as location is concerned. A variable named *tax, sum,* and *total* are all in different memory locations and the numeric location may not be consecutive. To address them you reference them by name. **Arrays** on the other hand are really neat in that they are *sequential areas of memory that hold like data.* So, you might have three areas, all next to each other, that had the same name, but each area in the array held, for example, integer data, and the specific position, in the same-named array variable is indexed via an index position.

This index position starts with 0 (zero) and ends at the last addressable spot, which is 1 - the length of the array. For an array which had three elements in it, the addressable positions would be 0 - 2. Try out what follows to see how it works with very simple array. In the example an array is created, and data is later put into it, and printed from it.

First let's examine a single dimension array, the simplest type.

```
//A very simple single dimension array
#include<iostream>
using namespace std;

int main()
{
        int simple_array[3]; // create an array of integer type with three elements
        simple_array[0]=1; // put data into the first position  0  1  2
        simple_array[1]=2;
        simple_array[2]=simple_array[0]+ simple_array[1]; // add two positions, store in third
        cout << simple_array[0];
        cout << simple_array[1];
        cout << simple_array[2]  << endl;

        system("pause");
        return 0;
}
```

With the previous example, you declared an array that was three elements long, with no values in the elements (they are empty). Next data was placed into the integer array and later displayed to the screen.

Next, let's create an array with an *initializer list of data*. In this fashion the array will be sized by the amount of data you wish to put in it. Note there are two examples to see how this works.

```cpp
//A very simple single dimension array with initializer list, initializer list determines size of array
#include<iostream>
using namespace std;

int main()
{
        int simple_array[] = {1,2,3,7,2};  // create an array of integer type and pre-set data in
                                           // elements
                                           //note no size is given to the array..is is sized by the
                                           //list!
        cout << simple_array[0];  // prints 1
        cout << simple_array[1];  // prints 2
        cout << simple_array[2];  // prints 3
        cout << simple_array[3];  // prints 7
        cout << simple_array[4]  << end;  // prints 2

        system("pause");
        return 0;
}
```

```cpp
//A very simple single dimension array with initializer list and only one item initialized
#include<iostream>
using namespace std;

int main()
{
        int simple_array[5] = { 0,0,0,7,0 };  // only set 4th element to 7 the rest are zero

        cout << simple_array[0] << endl;  // prints 0
        cout << simple_array[1] << endl;  // prints 0
        cout << simple_array[2] << endl;  // prints 0
        cout << simple_array[3] << endl;  // prints 7
        cout << simple_array[4] << endl;  // prints 0

        system("pause");
        return 0;
}
```

Next, let's set a constant for the array size, and allow the user to enter some data.

```cpp
//User input with a single dimensional array
#include<iostream>
using namespace std;

int const SIZE = 3;

int main()
{
char simple_array[SIZE];   // create three element array of characters

cout << "Enter three characters, separated by a space, and I will reverse them: "<< endl;

cin >> simple_array[0] >> simple_array[1] >> simple_array[2];

cout << " Here they are:  " << simple_array[2] << simple_array[1] << simple_array[0] << endl;

system("pause");
return 0;

}
```

Arrays using the array library

What we just examined were pre-C++ 11 or C-style array declarations. Not to be left out though are C++ versions 11 and newer which have an array library which offers a bit of extra functionality over traditional arrays at the expense of an extra library include (which is nothing) and perhaps a tad bit less readable syntax...but not really as you will see.

This library offers considerably more power with functions such as built in comparison operators, bounds checking, auto-access to start and beginning points, tuple creation (a non-changable or *immutable* array as Python would consider it), direct swap function, etc.

Make sure you have a modern compiler/IDE application such as NetBeans or Visual Studio 2013 or higher, etc. There are many fine resources on the *inner web* or *little Internet* such as http://en.cppreference.com/w/cpp/container/array you can research for more information. Try the following examples for some examples on how the array library can be of benefit to any good zombie hunter.

```cpp
//arrays via the array class
#include <iostream>
#include <array>
using namespace std;

int main()
{
        const int size = 4;
        array <int, size> simpleArray;  // create an array of <type, size> and name

        for (int value = 0; value < simpleArray.size(); value++) // loop through values
        {   simpleArray[value] = 3 + value; // add 3 plus counter to each position
                cout << simpleArray[value] << "\n";   } // print 'um!
        system("pause");
        return 0;
}
```

Note that the array-class version is not bad, and in fact a bit of research on the language standard will show there are quite a few interesting features of the array class.

```cpp
// more arrays via the array class
#include <iostream>
#include <array>
using namespace std;
void print_it(int x)
        {   cout << x << "\n";   }

int main()
{
        const int size = 4;
        array <int, size> simpleArray = { 9, 8, 7, 6 };  // create an array of <type, size> and name
//with initializer list
        for (int n : simpleArray)  // enhanced for to get through array
                print_it(n);

        system("pause");
        return 0;
}
```

```cpp
// Yet more with the array class
#include <iostream>
#include <array>
using namespace std;
void print_it(int x)
```

```
{   cout << x << "\n";   }

int main()
{
        const int size = 4;
        array <int, size> simpleArray = { 9, 8, 7, 6 };  // create an array of <type, size> and name
// with initializer list
        for (int n : simpleArray)  // enhanced for to get through array
                print_it(n);

        simpleArray.fill(7); // fill array with 7's

        for (int n : simpleArray)  // show 7's now
                print_it(n);

        system("pause");
        return 0;
}
```

The previous example is really neat since it shows an *enhanced for* loop (a loop which "knows" its own length) and a way to fill the array with some initial data. Next consider some of the other features of the array class. They "know" where the beginning and end of the array are.

```
// Example of the array class function to create a simple
// array 5 elements long and utilize the begin and end functions
#include <array>
#include <iostream>
using namespace std;

int main()
{
        const int array_size = 5;

        array <int, array_size> zombie_raid;

        for (int z = 0; z < array_size; z++)
           zombie_raid[z] = z + 1;

        for_each(zombie_raid.begin(), zombie_raid.end(), [](int num)
        {   cout << num << " at element: "  << num -1 << '\n';
           cout << "next line....\n";   } );

        system("pause");
        return 0;   }
```

90

The previous example shows that it can be handy to have the array "know" where it starts and ends. The *begin()* and *end()* iterator functions give this access. *At, front,* and *back* give access to a specific element, the first, and the last element. Try the following to see it in action.

```cpp
// Example of the array class functions
//at,front and back functions
#include <array>
#include <iostream>
using namespace std;

int main()
{
        const int array_size = 5;
        array <int, array_size> numbers;

        for (int n = 0; n < array_size; n++)
        {       numbers[n] = n + 1;
                cout << " " << numbers[n] << "--";
        }

        cout << endl << numbers.at(2) << endl; // print third elemnet
        cout << numbers.front() << "\n"; // print first element
        cout << numbers.back() << "\n"; // print the last element

        system("pause");

        return 0;
}
```

In the previous example we choose the third element (2) and the first (front) and back (last) positions. In the next example we will consider the fill and swap functions. These will fill an array with a specific value and swap one array for another.

```cpp
// Example of fill and swap operations
// fill is a form of null initializer
//swap does direct swap without the need for a third temp
//variable holder area
#include <string>
#include <array>
#include <iostream>
using namespace std;

int main()
```

```cpp
{
        array <int, 3> numbers = { 1, 3, 2 };
        cout << "Original values:\n";

        for (int value : numbers)
                cout << value; // print original values

        cout << "\nNow the changed values:\n";

        numbers.fill(2); // fill all element with 2

        for (int value : numbers)
                cout << value;  // print new array with only 2

        cout << "\nNow the swap function\n";

        array<string, 3> my_string_a = { string ("a "), "b ", "peanut" };
        array<string, 3> my_string_b = { string("c "), "d ", "zombie" };

        cout << "Original string a\n";
        for (string letter : my_string_a)
                cout << letter;  // print new array with only 2

        cout << endl;
        cout << "Original string b\n";
        for (string letter : my_string_b)
                cout << letter;  // print new array with only 2

        cout << endl;
        my_string_a.swap(my_string_b); // the old swap-O-rama

        cout << "New string a\n";
        for (string letter : my_string_a)
                cout << letter;  // print new array with only 2

        cout << endl;
        cout << "New string b\n";
        for (string letter : my_string_b)
                cout << letter;  // print new array with only 2

        cout << endl;

        system("pause");

        return 0;
}
```

Next let's examine arrays which have rows and columns, or multi-dimensional arrays.

Multi-dimensional arrays

Now that you have seen several ways to make single dimension arrays, you will want to consider multi-dimensional arrays. If you have ever seen a spreadsheet, with rows and columns, then think no further if you are trying to imagine an array. Instead of one row, with many columns, just consider both many rows and columns. These are just as easy to implement as what you finished earlier, you only need to add in the row counter. In the graphic which follows, note that you have an array named foo with *[row size] [column size]*.

For an array named foo	*col 0*	*col 1*	*col 2*	*col 3*
row 0	**foo[0][0]**	**foo[0][1]**	**foo[0][2]**	**foo[0][3]**
row 1	**foo[1][0]**	**foo[1][1]**	**foo[1][2]**	**foo[1][3]**
row 2	**foo[2][0]**	**foo[2][1]**	**foo[2][2]**	**foo[2][3]**

Figure 6.1 arrangement of rows and columns for multi-dimensional array.

Declaring this array is similar to a single dimension array. Follow along to see how.

```
//multi dimensional array without array library include
#include <iostream>
using namespace std;

int main()
{
        int zombie_array[3][4];
        for (int row = 0; row < 3; row++)
        {
                for (int col = 0; col < 4; col++)
                {   zombie_array[row][col] = 3; // put 3 in every element
                        cout << zombie_array[row][col] << " ";    }

                cout << endl;
                }
        system("pause");
        return 0;
}
```

This example created a 3x4 array and put 3 into each element. Try the next example to use an initializer list. Note initializer lists work the same with multi-dimensional arrays as single dimension arrays. This is a list of data you *initially* want in the array (but of course you already knew that!). Try the next example to see how it works.

```
//multi dimensional array without array library include
#include<iostream>
using namespace std;

int main()
{
            int myarray[3][4] = {
            { 1, 11, 6, 8 },  /*  initializer list for row 0 */
            { 3, 4, 6, 5 },  /*  initializer list for row 1 */
            { 2, 9, 99, 3 }   };            /*  row 2 */

     for (int row = 0; row < 3; row++)
     {
            for (int col = 0; col < 4; col++)
                    cout << myarray[row][col] << " ";
            cout << endl;    }

     system("pause");
     return 0;
}
```

Next, we should consider some other containers that any good computer scientist should be aware of. There are others, and you should examine the enhanced Boost libraries, and others. However, let's next look at a few other handy containers.

Lists

If you want to store the same data types (e.g. all *int*) then a *list* is a good choice. *Lists* are containers that store data in sequential memory locations. Lists are good for times when you need to insert, move, and remove elements. Additionally, they have a great many member functions, so a *list* might well be your first container choice after an array just based on what you can do with them that is built-in.

A *list* lacks direct access to elements by index position and use more memory when compared to arrays or vectors. Lists are stored in contiguous memory areas, like arrays, and do not allow random access to elements. Size is set when the list is created, though elements may change. Try the next example to see a *list* in action.

```cpp
//using a list in C++
#include <iostream>
#include <list>
using namespace std;

int main()
{
        list<int> my_list = { 2, 4, 6, 8 };        // our first list

        for (int n : my_list)
                cout << n << " ";

        cout << "\n\n"; // print original list

        my_list.push_front(1); // Add an integer to the front of the list

        for (int n : my_list) // print with 1 in front now
                cout << n << " ";

                cout<< "\n\n";

        my_list.push_back(9); // Add an integer to the end of our list

        for (int n : my_list)
                cout << n << " ";

        cout << "\n";
        // Insert an integer before 4
        auto temp_list = find(my_list.begin(), my_list.end(), 4);
        if (temp_list != my_list.end())
                my_list.insert(temp_list, 3);

        for (int n : my_list)  //print the final list
                cout << n << " ";

        cout << "\n";
        system("pause");  // hold screen open on Windows systems
        return 0;   }
```

Vectors

Stored in contiguous areas of memory and holding the same type of data (e.g. all char data) vectors are like an array but can change size. Vectors allow random access to elements and are efficient with regards to memory. Moving data around in a *vector* is not this containers strong point when comparing it to a *list*.

```cpp
//Using a vector C++
#include <iostream>
#include <vector>
using namespace std;

int main()
{
        // Create a vector containing integers
        vector<int> my_vec = { 1, 2, 3, 4, 5 };

        cout << my_vec.at(0) << endl << endl; //   Show first element position 0
        // Print values of orig vector
        cout << "Orig values in my_vec:\n";
        for (int counter : my_vec)
                cout << counter << '\n';

        my_vec.push_back(6); // append a 5 to the end

                cout << "Loop through revised vector:\n";
        // Print values of the revised vector
        for (int counter : my_vec)
                cout << counter << '\n';

        system("pause");
        return 0;   }
```

Tuples

In the Python language, *tuples* are *immutable* (not changeable) structures that hold different data types. As such in C++ you have some very nice container options with *tuples* in that you can have a mix of data in the container (*int, char*, etc). They are not changeable after you create them (if you flag them with the const qualifier), and the elements are accessed by their order in the container. The access must be a constant expression however, and not a variable though. So in the first example below where you see *get<0>(tuple_2)* the first element, *0* could not be an integer variable such as *counter*.

```cpp
// Very simple example of a tuple
#include <iostream>
#include <tuple>
#include <string>
using namespace std;

int main()
{
        // first tuple declared constant to make immutable
        const tuple<int, string> total_apples_1(10, "apple");  // first element is 0 second is 1
        tuple<int, string> tuple_2(total_apples_1);  // copy first tuple to second

        cout << get<1>(total_apples_1) << endl; // print second element 1

        cout << get<0>(tuple_2) << endl; // print first element 0

        get<0>(tuple_2) = 3;
        get<1>(tuple_2) = "pears";

        cout << get<0>(tuple_2) << endl; // now print changes first element
        cout << get<1>(tuple_2) << endl; // now print changes second element
        //Note that the numeric value behind get requires a constant expression
        //and not a variable such as with a loop, so using a for to get
        //elements is not an option with the standard library

        cout << tuple_2._Mysize << endl;  // so tuple_2 is 2 in length (2 elements)

        system("pause");
        return 0;   }
```

In the next example we will unpack a tuple into a few individual variables. The tie function will help us with this.

```cpp
//Tuple example 2
//Create a tuple, change an element
//uppack tuple with tie to individual variables and print
#include <iostream>
#include <tuple>
#include <string>
using namespace std;
```

```cpp
int main()
{
        int age;
        char middle_inital;
        string last_name;

        // declare a tuple
        tuple<int, char, string> tuple_1(0, ' ', "blank");

        get<2>(tuple_1) = "Fred";

        //use tie to unpack tuples to individual variables
        tie(age, middle_inital, last_name) = tuple_1;

        cout << "Data as follows -- " << endl;
        cout << "Age:  " << age << endl;
        cout << "Middle inital:  " << middle_inital << endl;
        cout << "Last name: " << last_name << endl;

        system("pause");
        return 0;   }
```

This chapter covered many topics, some such as tuples, lists, and vectors get much more involved as you may well imagine. Take what you have learned and expand your learning with the exercises which follow.

Notes to remember

Learning extension

1) Create an array for grades for a test for a class with 10 students. Input the grades via console input, and print out each of the numeric grades.

2) Create a program which uses a vector to store sales for several salesmen as integers. Output the data to the screen for each salesman.

3) Create a tuple with data a pet store might use. Unpack and print the data.

4) Using the second tuple example, complete modifiers for age and middle initial. Perhaps use cin and allow user interaction.

5) Create a tuple which represents a pet. Include name, age, breed or type, and condition of health. You should have integer, floating point, character data at the least.

6) Create a tuple which represents a student. Include GPA, major, last name, first name, and phone.

7) A car dealership uses a list to store car sales. Create a list of sales for the day, then add a sale during the middle of the day (middle of the list) which unfortunately was not accounted for until after the initial list was created. Print the before and after list. Allow the user to enter the new sales record to the list (e.g. prompt the user for this new sale).

8) Using *Intellisense*, examine and implement two other features which a list offers. Be explicit and use comments to explain your work.

9) Using *Intellisense*, examine and implement two other features which a vector offers. Be explicit and use comments to explain your work.

10) For problem 1, use a 10 point scale and convert the final numeric output for each grade to a letter, such as A, B, C, etc.

Chapter 7

Structures, Exception handling, Enumerations,

Address of operator and Pointers

Soon you will learn about OOP or Object Orient Programming, which is a way to create objects (which for now let's consider as new variables) from a pre-defined model that you define. This model might be a person (with features such as last name, first name, age, etc) or a car (with features such as cylinders, color, number of doors, etc) or any other noun-type thing. Any good zombie hunter knows you have to take certain things for granted (such as why the zombie apocalypse started) and just shoot zombies and survive. Let's leave OOP for a later chapter and keep the concept of creating these reusable structures simple for now. As a matter of fact, *strucs* are almost the same as OOP objects, until you get to some extra features they offer. Until that chapter, enter the Stuct(ure) zone!.

Structures

Starting with the C language, which did not support OOP, the authors needed a way to create these reusable structures from a model. The *struct* or structure was this feature. A *struct* is a process in which you can make your own data type structures. In fact OOP design has this process, albeit it is much more advanced, but the general concept in a light-weight fashion can be accomplished on some levels with *structs*.

The C language, far from being dead, is used in device programming, such as with electronics or robotics. This is due in large part since with programming these types of devices, OOP is not needed. Applications programmers however will find that C++ offers more power. However rest assured if you learn one, the other is exceptionally similar, such that you can easily switch between the two. If you can shoot an AK-47 you can shoot an AR-15...most would argue there has never been a zombie who has complained afterwards!

If you think about an *int* or *string* as data types, imagine that you might have some data structure that encompasses both *int's* and *string's*, or more to make a complete data structure.

Try a *struct* out

Consider for example that you had some structure named STUDENT which had a name, gpa, age, etc. Keyword *struct* and a valid variable-type name creates a *struct*, with of course any members you require. The following example will show how this works. Run it, (after adding what you need to add noted in the comments for student 2).

```cpp
//Example 1 of a structure or struct
#include <iostream>
#include <string>
using namespace std;

struct STUDENT {   // Declare STUDENT as a struct data type
        string name;   //Members
        int age;
        char grade_level; //f ror freshmen, s for sophomore, j for junior or s for senior
        float gpa;    // 4.0 max highest
        }; // note there is a semi colon here!...this is only used with structs and
        classes!

int main()
{
        STUDENT student1;   // create first data type based on student struct
        STUDENT student2;  //create second based on student struct

        student1.name = "Fred";  // pre-assign student 1 name with format:
                                 // structure.member name    student1.name

        cout << "Please enter student 2's name: ";
        cin >> student2.name;

        student1.age = 18;
        student2.age = 44;
        student1.gpa = 4.0;
        student2.gpa = 3.0;
        //note structure.name goes both ways...you can set or get data as what follows:

        cout << student1.name << " is " << student1.age << " old with a GPA of " <<
student1.gpa << endl;
        // you finish code for student 2 here....

        system("pause");
        return 0;
}
```

Hands-on: Finish student 2

So, as in the comments, after you run this code, finish the information for student 2 and re-run it.
You could easily copy what you did for the *cout* for student1 , paste and change it to be student2.
Experiment with more changes if you really feel you are on a roll! Next, let's examine a *struct*
for a pet data structure.

```
//Example 2 of a struct about your pets
#include <iostream>
#include <string>
using namespace std;

struct PET
{   string pet_name;
        int pet_age;
        string breed;
};

int main()
{
        PET pet1;

        cout << "Enter your pet name:  ";
        cin >> pet1.pet_name;
        cout << "Enter your pet age:  ";
        cin >> pet1.pet_age;
        cout << "Breed of pet? ";
        cin >> pet1.breed;
        cout << pet1.pet_name << " is " << pet1.pet_age << " old and is this breed: " <<
pet1.breed << endl;

        system("pause");
        return 0;
}
```

Next let's consider zombie types with a struct.

```
//Example for zombie types
#include <iostream>
#include <string>
using namespace std;

struct zombie
{
```

```cpp
        string zombie_name;
        int age;
        string zombie_type;
};

int main()
{
        zombie zombie_1;

        cout << "Enter zombie name:  ";
        cin >> zombie_1.zombie_name;
        cout << "Enter your zombie age: ";
        cin >> zombie_1.age;
        cout << "Type (e.g. dog, human, pig, etc.?: ";
        cin >> zombie_1.zombie_type;
        cout << zombie_1.zombie_name << " is " << zombie_1.age << " years old.  The type of
zombie is: " << zombie_1.zombie_type << endl;

        system("pause");
        return 0;
}
```

And one last struct. Next let's add in a vampire struct.

```cpp
#include<iostream>
using namespace std;

struct zombie
{
        int limbs;
        int hunger_level;
        bool recent_dead;
}; // note semicolon to mark end

struct vampire
{
        int limbs;
        bool day_walker;
        bool wings;
}; // again mark end

int main()
{
        zombie sara;
        vampire vlad;

        sara.hunger_level = 10;
```

```
        sara.limbs = 3;
        sara.recent_dead = 0;
        vlad.limbs = 4;
        vlad.day_walker = 1;
        vlad.wings = 0;

        cout << "Limbs  Hunger Level  Recently Dead as bool" << endl;
cout << sara.limbs  << "      "  << sara.hunger_level  << "      "  << sara.recent_dead << endl;

        cout << "Limbs  Day Walker  Wings as bool" << endl;
        cout << vlad.limbs << "      " << vlad.day_walker << "           " << vlad.wings << endl;

        system("pause");
        return 0;
}
```

Exception handling with *try* and *catch*

Exception handling is important since once you had a program working, you would want to "user proof" it or make it such that if the user entered some incorrect value, or for whatever reason the program encountered a problem, then it would not crash but, in a best-case situation, would report exactly what happened to the user. This could be reported back to the program creator for further refinement or help. Consider the next example where a 1 is returned if the user entered a 0. Think that the *try* is like an *if*, it is looking for truth that it can run the code segment, the *catch* is the *else*, in other words the *if* is not true or possible, so a false (*catch*) condition is met.

```
//Example Error handling #1
#include <iostream>
using namespace std;

int main()
{
        int x;
        cout << "Enter a pos integer: ";
        cin >> x;
        try
        {
                if (x == 0)
                        throw 1;

                cout << "number entered * 10 is: " << x * 10 << endl;
        }
        catch (int err_code)
```

104

```
        {
                cout << "ERROR CODE " << err_code << " you entered a 0" << endl;
        }

        system("pause");
        return 0;
}
```

Use error handling (or add it) after you have your code running. It might not be best to worry about adding in error handling code during your first attempt(s) at getting your code running. However, feel free, if it fits your coding style, to add it during prototyping. Either way though you will want to go back through your code and "user" proof it with error handling.

Writing and Reading files

So far we have dealt with data that does not last beyond when we last ran the program. Or put another way, anything we did was only stored in RAM (Random Access Memory) and was not stored in some persistent, long-term method such as in the format of a file on a hard drive, DVD, etc (the source file was but not any date from when the program ran such as a high score). Enter the concept of *persistent data*, or writing and reading data with files. It is *persistent* since it is stored on the hard drive, and not lost in RAM when the program closes. For example, if you start a game, the previous high score or last login ID might be displayed, and that data would have been stored persistently and not only in temporary RAM memory.

So, when you worked with console input or output (*cin* or *cout*) you were reading from the console or writing to the console. With files, consider that you can read and write from a file stream, instead (or in addition to) of the keyboard and console. The process is so similar to what you already know you will find it super easy. The big difference? It only takes a few library includes and a check to make sure your file can be opened/exists/can be read/written. Consider the following:

Reading and writing to files is a key part of programming you should know how to do. Consider a game where when the game starts it displays the most recent high score. This is a program that looks for a data file, reads it, and….shows the last high score that was saved. If you consider reading and writing from the keyboard (cin) and to the monitor (cout) then you have the concept, just consider reading or writing from or to a file. Easy!

105

What follows is a simple example to take a bit of user input, and save it to a file. If you are usng M.S. Visual Studio, it will create a text file in the project folder directory. Use notepad or your favorite text editor to read it.

```
//write to a file very simple...no error handling
#include<iostream>
#include<fstream>
#include<string>
using namespace std;

int main()
{
        ofstream outfile("mydead.txt", ios::out);
        string number, undead;
        int score;
        int cont = 0;

        while (cont < 1)
        {
        cout << "Enter Number, Undead name, & health score from 0 - 10 such as 1 Brown 6:  ";
        cin >> number >> undead >> score;
        outfile << number << "  " << undead << "  " << score << endl;
        cout << " Next?: " << endl;
        cout << "Continue? 0 if yes or 1 to exit: ";
        cin >> cont;
        }
        system("pause");
        return 0;     }
```

After you run this, open the project folder and you will find the text file it created called "mydead.txt" that will have the information you entered. Use Notepad or your favorite word Processing application to open the file and see your plain text data. Of course you can specify a specific path to another location, just make sure you have rights to write to that area. Also note DOS and UNIX have different directory markers (slash faces different directions) and UNIX (Linux and Mac OS) do not use drive letter designations as DOS (Windows) does.

In the next example we will create a very super simple example that just writes a user's first and last name to a text file. The file name is first_last.txt so open that, from the directory where the project is save, with your favorite text editor to see the first and last name.

```
//write first and last name to a file
#include<iostream>
#include<fstream>
#include<string>
using namespace std;

int main()
{
        ofstream outfile("first_last.txt", ios::out);
        string first, last;
        int cont = 0;
        cout << "Enter first name:  ";
        cin >> first;
        cout << "Enter last name:  ";
        cin >> last;
        outfile << first << "  " << last << "  " << endl;
        cout << "Now open with a text editor the file first_last.txt" << endl;
        system("pause");
        return 0;
}
```

Now let's change what we just wrote to include error handling. This would be important since if you did not have rights to create the file or there was not enough disk space it would crash so hopefully the *try/except* will handle that.

```
//write first and last name to a file
#include<iostream>
#include<fstream>
#include<string>
using namespace std;

int main()
{
        try {
                ofstream outfile("first_last.txt", ios::out);
                string first, last;
                cout << "Enter first name:  ";
                cin >> first;
                cout << "Enter last name:  ";
                cin >> last;
                outfile << first << "  " << last << "  " << endl;
                cout << "Now open with your favorite text editor the file first_last.txt" << endl;
        }
        catch (...) {
                cout << "Could not create file, exiting....";
```

```
            system("exit");
      }
      system("pause");
      return 0;
}
```

Does the extension have to be *txt*? No! You could make one with an *htm* or *html* extension, or whatever you wish. However, naming them *exe*, xls, or *doc*, etc. would be bad form. Stick to extensions which are for text files. Try another example to see this in action.

```
//Write a zombie name to a file
#include<iostream>
#include<fstream>
#include<string>
using namespace std;

int main()
{       //create output file stream object and file name
        ofstream out_name("name.txt", ios::out);

        string name;
        cout << "Enter the name of the zombie\n";
        cin >> name;

        try // to write it to a file
        {
                out_name << name << "\n";
                cout << "file sucessfully written!\n";
                out_name.close();

        }
        catch (int e) // catch and display problem
        {
                cout << "Could not write it!\n" << e << endl;
        }

        system("pause");
        return 0;
}
```

In the previous example you included a new library to allow the creation of a file stream object. Declare it like a variable, then send data to it just like you would to the console! A big step to not forget though is to close the file stream. Not doing so will leave the file in an open state and

108

can cause file corruption. In the next example consider a more practical example where we write out sales values, stored in an array, to a file. Definitely a neat example.

```cpp
#include<iostream>
#include<fstream>
using namespace std;

int main()
{
        ofstream outputsales("sales.txt", ios::out);

        int salesResults[5][6];  /// one size larger to keep #'s consistent

        for (int salesMen = 1; salesMen <= 4; salesMen++)
        {
                for (int products = 1; products <= 5; products++)
                {
                        cout << "For salesmen #" << salesMen << "how many sold of product " << products << " ?" << endl;
                        cin >> salesResults[salesMen][products];

                }

        }

        for (int totals = 1; totals <= 4; totals++)
        {
                cout << "Salesperson # " << totals << " sold " << endl;
                for (int p = 1; p <= 5; p++)
                {       cout << salesResults[totals][p] << " Item # " << p << " --- ";
                        // write to file as well
                        outputsales << salesResults[totals][p] << " Item # " << p << " --- ";
                }
                outputsales << endl;  // write to file also
                cout << endl;
        }
        system("pause");
        return 0;
}
```

After writing data, you will want to read it back into your programs. This is as similar as using an input file in place of *cin* for console input. A key important point is to check that the file can be read. Rights, incorrect directories, or a Zombie Apocalypse can cause these issues so just check for them as noted in the next example.

```cpp
/Read a zombie name from a file
#include<fstream>
#include<string>
#include<iostream>
using namespace std;

int main()
{       //create output file stream object and file name
        ofstream out_name("name.txt", ios::out);

        string name;
        cout << "Enter a first name for the zombie\n";
        cin >> name;
        //write it out!
        try // to write it to a file
        {
                out_name << name << "\n";
                cout << "file sucessfully written!\n";
                out_name.close();

        }
        catch (int e) // catch and display problem
        {
                cout << "Could not write it!\n" << e << endl;
        }
        //read it in
        ifstream in_name("name.txt", ios::in);
        if (!in_name) {
                cerr << "Unable to open file!";
                exit(1);   // exit with error
        }
        else
        {
                string data;
                in_name >> data;
                cout << data  << endl;
        }
        cout << "\nThe end!\n";
        in_name.close();
        system("pause");
        return 0;
}
```

Next, note some changes that allow for words, not just one, to be written and read. Try it out.

```cpp
//Read zombie names from a file
#include<fstream>
#include<string>
#include<iostream>
using namespace std;

int main()
{       //create output file stream object and file name
        ofstream out_name("name.txt", ios::out);

        string name;
        cout << "Enter a first and last name for the zombie\n";
        getline(cin, name);

        //write it out!
        try // to write it to a file
        {
                out_name << name << "\n";
                cout << "file sucessfully written!\n";
                out_name.close();

        }
        catch (int e) // catch and display problem
        {
                cout << "Could not write it!\n" << e << endl;
        }
        //read it in
        ifstream in_name("name.txt", ios::in);
        if (!in_name) {
                cerr << "Unable to open file!";
                exit(1);   // exit with error
        }
        else
        {       // read all data not just one word!
                string data;
                while (getline(in_name, data))
                {
                        cout << data  << endl;
                }

        }
        cout << "\nThe end!\n";
        in_name.close();
        system("pause");
        return 0;
}
```

Challenge:

The aforementioned example named a file with a txt extension. Rename it (in code of course) to *htm* and open the file you create with the program using a web browser. Note the format.

Enumerations

Enumerations are a data type where each word is representative of a numeric value, where the name makes more sense to represent the number. If you think about days in the week, or months in a year, Jan. would be a 1, Feb. a 2, etc. However, representing something as "January" just makes more sense than to say the month is "1". With enumerations you can represent numbers with words and make your code much easier to read. They should be considered constants with regard to type, so don't plan on changing them. You may hear them referred to as "enumerators" but they are still the same. Try the examples below to see how they work.

```cpp
//Example a simple enum(eration)
#include <iostream>
using namespace std;

int main()
{
        enum days {mon, tues, wed, thurs, fri, sat, sun};
        days week1 = fri;

        switch (week1)
        {
        case mon:
                cout << "Monday";
                break;
        case tues:
                cout << "Tuesday\n";
                break;
        case wed:
                cout << "Wed\n";
                break;
        case thurs:
                cout << "Thursday\n";
                break;
        case fri:
                cout << "Friday, thank God!!!!\n";
                break;
```

112

```
        case sat:
                cout << "Saturday\n";
                break;
        case sun:
                cout << "Sunday\n";
                break;
        }
        system("pause");
        return 0;
}
```

Next let's try another enumeration example.

```
//Example a numeric enumeration
#include <iostream>
using namespace std;

int main()
{       //You can assign a positive or negative value for your enumerations.
        //Some can even have the same value...but be careful.
        //Then will increase in value from where you start if not explicitly assigned for non-
//negative values.
        enum Levels
        {       level_one = 1,
                level_two = 2,
                level_three  // Assigned 3
        };

        Levels my_level=level_three;
        cout << my_level << endl; // this will print a three

        system("pause");
        return 0;
}
```

Try one more examples with colors.

```
// enums with colors!
#include <iostream>
using namespace std;

int main()
{
        enum my_color { red=0, cyan=1, magenta=2 };
        cout << "Enter color -- 0 for red, 1 for cyan, 2 for magenta: ";
        int color;
        cin >> color;
```

```
switch (color)
{
case red:
cout << "Red hot!\n";
break;
case cyan:
cout << "Cyan blues!\n";
break;
case magenta: cout << "Magenta City!\n";
break;
default:
        cout << "no!";
}
system("pause");
return 0;
}
```

Casting

Casting is more fun if you are fishing, perhaps for zombie fish, but casting data from one type to another (e.g. from an integer to a float) is also handy and fun. It can take place automatically (implicitly) or explicitly when you tell it to. It is a *narrowing conversion if you go from more precise to less precise.* By the same logic, it is a *widening conversion if you go from less precise, e.g. an integer to a more precise floating point variable.* Try the simple example to see how we can narrow from more precise to less precise (float to integer) or widen precision (say character to string, integer to float, float to double, etc.)

```
//Simple casting
#include <iostream>
using namespace std;

int main()
{
        float a = 1.1;
        cout << int(a) << " Variable a narrow cast down to integer\n";

        int b = 8;
        cout << float(b) << " Integer b widened via casting to float\n";
        cout << "Add them up!\n";
        cout << a + b << " b var is implicitly promoted to float for math.\n";

        system("pause");
```

114

```
        return 0;
}
```

Address of operator and pointers

Now we will learn about pointing things to memory addresses and pointers to memory locations. The & operator in front of a variable will point to the address in memory (a memory cell location) of the variable. This is of course much smaller in size than a copy of it. Think of this is similar to a shortcut in Windows. As an example snippit:

```
        Orig_variable = 10;

        Copy_var = Orig_variable;  // copy the original into the copy

        Addr_orig = &Orig_variable;  // addr_orig has the address of where original is

        foo_bar = *Addr_orig;
```

So addr_orig is a *pointer* to Orig_variable and foo_bar (dereference operator) points to the data. So & is address of the operator and * is a pointer to the data. Note in the next example you will see how this works.

```
// Simple address of and pointers
#include <iostream>
using namespace std;

void main()
{
        int value1 = 1;
        int * num1;  // num1 is a pointer

        num1 = &value1;  // address of value1 is pointed to by num1
        cout << "value 1 data = " << value1 << "\n";
        cout << num1  << " memory address of num1 is a pointer to value 1!\n";  // output it

        *num1 = 999;        // value pointed to by num1= 999
        cout << num1 << " == " << value1 << " address and value\n";

        cout << "value 1 data now = 999 note-> " << *num1 << "\n";
        system("pause");
}
```

Using what you have learned, try the learning extension to expand your knowledge.

Notes to remember

Learning extension

1) Create a pet type with structs. Create at least three elements for each struct and a minimum of two structs. Output the results to the screen.

2) Create an application which narrows and widens variables. Output the results to the screen. Use as many examples as you can.

3) For student 2 where you were to complete the code, show your work here as a complete program.

4) Create a vampire type with structs. Allow for user input to add data to the struct. Four elements minimum for the struct.

5) Using the sample of how to create a file. Create a web page! Basic format for a web page is as follows:

```
<!DOCTYPE html>
<html>
<body>

<h1>first</h1>
<p>last</p>

</body>
</html>
```

Create an application which asks for first and last name and creates a web page with the associated information. Bonus if you visit W3schools to find other markup tags to add in!

6) Create an application which sorts via a switch statement for days of the week as enumerations.

7) Create an application which sorts via a switch statement for months of the year as enumerations.

8) Create a program that allows the user to enter numeric final grades, and assigns letter grades of A, B, C, etc. via a switch. User enumerations.

9) Create an enumeration-based program for a medical clinic. Use either the Wong-Baker ® scale or the one used by the VA (Veterans Administration).

10) Create a game based on the use of enumerations. Do not create a Craps game though as this has been done many times!

11) IPTV and M3U file lists for FTA and free IP tv are the rage! Just check out Kodi or OSMC and you will see. Create an application which allows you to make an IPTV XML or M3U file for use on one of them. It should allow the user to enter channel info and create a file which can be imported to one of the devices. This is easier than you think! Research formats first, then channel listings.

Chapter 8

Importing from other Libraries and Arrays

One thing you will often do in applications programming is work with string data. There are some great features built-in to C++ to work with strings. A consideration of primitive data types will reveal that strings or string variables are actually a compound variable, made up of individual character data. The #import <string> library allows you to work with string variables with ease.

Simple *string* library example

So, string data is actually a series of characters (each is a letter right?). In fact *strings* are really character arrays (which we will get to more formally in a moment). But, for now think of *strings* as a data type like integers, but you have to reference a library to get them to work. Names, colors, places, words, sentences, etc. are all examples of strings. You can access each character in a *string*, and *strings* have some really handy functions built into them. Let's try a bit with strings.

```cpp
// String example 1
#include <iostream>
#include<string>
using namespace std;

int main()
{
        string letters = "abc";
        cout << "First position 0 is: " << letters[0] << endl;

        cout << "Everything:  " << letters << endl;

        //Use enhanced for to loop through string
        for (char character : letters)
                cout << character;

        cout << "Next change first position by a letter\n";

        letters[0] = 'z' ; //change first position to a z
```

118

```
        cout << letters;  //show how changed by one position

        system("pause");
        return 0;
}
```

In the previous example, you created a string (and used the string library), addressed positions in the string, looped through the string with an enhanced *for* loop, and changed data in only one place in the string (from 'a' to a 'z'). Neat enough but you can do more. Note in the next example you can find things in a string, append to them, etc. When you type the stringname and . you will see that intellisense provides a dropdown with many more options that what is shown below. Try your hand at others as you see fit.

```
// Enter five unique values
#include <iostream>
#include <string>
using namespace std;

int main()
{
        string sentence= "I cannot see you!";
        cout << "Original string:  " << sentence << endl;

        cout << "Example of sub string\n";
        //get a sub string from the first position
        //up to but not including 4th position
        cout << sentence.substr(0, 4);

        cout << "\nNext example is append\n";
        //append to existing string
        sentence.append(" Unless I get a flashlight");

        cout << sentence << endl;
        cout << "\How long is that string in the window?: \n";
        cout << sentence.length() << " is the length.\n";

        //Next find the ! point location
        cout << "Find the !\n";
        int found_position = sentence.find("!");
        cout << "! found at position: " << found_position <<endl;
        system("pause");
        return 0;
}
```

Arrays

Arrays (and array-like structures) are sequential areas in memory which hold like data. Whoa! What does all that really mean? Actually, not much beyond the variables you already know, yet much more beyond. Let's dig in a bit.

So, when you create a variable, say Tax, then it is in an area of memory….auto assigned to a free area by the compiler. Have another, say Sum, and it will be assigned some free area in memory. These are addressable with ease as you know. However, looping through them requires giving the specific name of the variable, and each variable. With arrays you have one common name for the series of variables, but different index numbers for each position or "cell" in the array of several values. Consider that you might have an array named *values*, with four cells of data, accessing each position requires the common name, values, and a position. E.g. values[0] to get to the first position (you start with 0 and not 1). Think of one row, with several columns of data and you have a single dimension array. We'll get to multi-dimension arrays in a bit.

First, let's examine an old, but certainly valid, style array example. After using the old-style arrays we will use the new C++14 style, however both work the same way. First is a four element array, where we get user input for data, load data in via code, and show that arrays are not pre-initialized so you need to do this before using an array cell location in memory.

```cpp
#include<iostream>
using namespace std;

int main()
{
        int my_array[4];
        // array positions are 0 - 3
        // put 2 in first position
        my_array[0] = 2;
        // ask user to enter second data elements
        cout <<"Enter a value for second element: ";
        cin >> my_array[1];  // get data from user
        //Print them out
        for (int item : my_array)
                cout << item << endl;

        cout <<"Note last two data items were not initialized only a --memory address prints!";

        system("pause");
```

```
        return 0;
}
```

Note that the last example used an **enhanced** *for* statement. Nice eh? The next does not, but does use an **initializer list** which initializes the size of the array automatically. The size of the data determines the size of the array. Try it out.

```
#include<iostream>
using namespace std; // example with initializer list to size array

int main()
{
        int my_array[] = { 1,2,3,4 };
        // array positions are 0 - 3
        // filled via initializer list
        //Print them out via traditional for loop
        for (int item = 0; item < 4; item++)
                cout << my_array[item] << endl;

        system("pause");
        return 0;
}
```

Lastly, let us try a **character array** (like a string as you have probably guessed). Note the use again of an enhanced array though a traditional *while* or *for* would have worked.

```
#include<iostream>
using namespace std;

int main()
{
        char my_array[] = { 'a','b' ,'c' };
        // array positions are 0 - 2
        // filled via initializer list
        //Print them out via enhanced for
        for (char item : my_array)
        cout << item << endl;
        cout <<"Now you know your ABC's!\n";
        system("pause");
        return 0;
}
```

For a bit more fun, let's try an example which only stores unique values in an array.

```cpp
// Enter five unique values
#include <iostream>
using namespace std;

int main()
{
        int numbers[5];
        for (int value=0; value < 5; value++)
                numbers[value] = 0;  // zero the array out


        cout << "Enter 5 unique values 1-100: " << endl;
        cout << "Enter the same one twice and I will not store it!";
        cin >> numbers[0];  // first value is cool, store it
        int counter = 1;
        int check_value;
        int go = 0;

        while (counter < 5) // get four more and check against array
        {                                       //but only run to the value of the  counter for speed
                cout << "Enter 4 more unique values 1-100: " << endl;
                cout << "Enter the same one twice and I will not store it!";
                cin >> check_value;

                for (int run = 0; run < counter; run++) // counter increases as we move fwd.
                {
                        if (numbers[run] == check_value)
                        {
                                cout << "\nI already have that value!" << endl;
                                run = 5;
                                go = 0;
                        }
                        else
                                go = 1;
                }

                if (go == 1)
                {
                        numbers[counter] = check_value;
                        cout << "\nStored the value" << endl;
                        counter += 1;
                }
        } // end while

        //Use enhanced for to show the values
```

```cpp
        for (int values : numbers)
                cout << values  << endl;

        system("pause");
        return 0;
}
```

The previous example used several types of looping structures. Neat eh? In this next example we have ten salespeople who we want to calculate sales for.

```cpp
#include<iostream>
using namespace std;
//salespeople sales totals
int main()
{
        int sales[10] = { 0, 0, 0, 0, 0, 0, 0, 0, 0, 0 };
        // declare a 10 element array    -- 1 - 9 and skip position 0
        // name array sales[10]   0 is skipped 1 - 9 used

        int run = 0;  // loop counter indefinite loop

        while (run != -1)
        {
                cout << "Enter sales amount or -1 to exit: " << endl;
                cin >> run;

                if (run >= 200 && run <= 299)
                        sales[1] += 1;

                else if (run >= 300 && run <= 399)
                        sales[2] += 1;

                else if (run >= 400 && run <= 499)
                        sales[3] += 1;

                else if (run >= 500 && run <= 599)
                        sales[4] += 1;

                else if (run >= 600 && run <= 699)
                        sales[5] += 1;

                else if (run >= 700 && run <= 799)
                        sales[6] += 1;

                else if (run >= 800 && run <= 899)
```

```cpp
                sales[7] += 1;

        else if (run >= 900 && run <= 999)
                sales[8] += 1;

        else if (run >= 1000)
                sales[9] += 1;
        else
                cout << " Not valid!" << endl;

}       // print the sales
cout << "There were " << sales[1] << " salespeople" << " in the $200 to $299 range\n";
cout << "There were " << sales[2] << " salespeople" << " in the $300 to $399 range\n";
cout << "There were " << sales[3] << " salespeople" << " in the $400 to $499 range\n";
cout << "There were " << sales[4] << " salespeople" << " in the $500 to $599 range\n";
cout << "There were " << sales[5] << " salespeople" << " in the $600 to $699 range\n";
cout << "There were " << sales[6] << " salespeople" << " in the $700 to $799 range\n";
cout << "There were " << sales[7] << " salespeople" << " in the $800 to $899 range\n";
cout << "There were " << sales[8] << " salespeople" << " in the $900 to $999 range\n";
cout << "There were " << sales[9] << " salespeople" << " 1000 or higher!\n";

        system("pause");
        return 0;
}
```

Multi-dimensional arrays

What we have used so far are single dimension arrays. You certainly can have two dimensional arrays. Consider a checkerboard or spreadsheet and you have a good idea. Rows and columns, with the intersection point being where your cell of data is. What follows below is a super-simple 2x2 array which allows you to replace the zero with a numeric value of your choice.

```cpp
#include<iostream>
using namespace std;

int main()
{
        int my_data[2][2] = { 1, 2, 3, 0 };

        cout << my_data[0][0] << endl;

        cout << "Enter data for cell 1,1";
        cin >> my_data[1][1];
        cout << "you input " << my_data[1][1] << endl;
```

124

```
        system("pause");
        return 0;    }
```

Challenge: Change the code to be a 3x3 array and put data in the last cell position via user input.

Next let's examine a multi-dimensional array which provides data on zombie hunters and how many kills versus misses they have had.

```
//data on zombie hunters and how many kills vs misses
#include<iostream>
using namespace std;

#define hunters 3
#define kills_misses 2

int main()
{
        int z_data[hunters][kills_misses];

        z_data[0][0] = 9; // hunter 0 9 kills
        z_data[0][1] = 1; // hunter 0 1 misses
        z_data[1][0] = 5; //hunter 1 5 kills
        z_data[1][1] = 2; //hunter 1 2 misses
        z_data[2][0] = 3; //hunter 2 3 kills
        z_data[2][1] = 0; //hunter 2 0 misses

        for (int hunter=0; hunter <3; hunter++) // 0, 1, 2 hunters!
        {
                cout << z_data[hunter][0] << " Kills" << endl;
                cout << z_data[hunter][1] << " Misses" << endl;
        }

        system("pause");
        return 0;
}
```

So, we have made single dimension and jagged, ragged, or multi-dimensional arrays. Next let's consider that there is a array class, as of C++ 14 and higher, which adds functionality, though you may not need it. Regardless, we will examine how the newer array class works and some of the added features.

Using the *array class* library to make a simple array

What follows is a simple array, but using the array class library. Note these arrays have a bit more "knowledge" about themselves. Such as they can be sorted, know their own length, you can insert data at certain points, delete it, etc.

```
//data on zombie hunters and weapons via array class library
#include<iostream>
#include <string>
#include <array>
using namespace std;

//#define hunters 3
int main()
        {
                array<int, 3> hunters = { 5, 9, 7 };
                array<int, 3> weapons = { 11, 12, 2 };

                // sort hunters
                sort(hunters.begin(), hunters.end());

                cout << '\n';

                // ranged for loop is supported
                for (int h : hunters)
                        cout << h << " is a hunter\n";
                cout << "Note the array is sorted now!\n";
                cout << "For each of the three hunters, their weapons are:\n";
                for (int w : weapons)
                        cout << w << " is their weapon type\n";

        system("pause");
        return 0;
}
```

The format is a bit different, but the array process works the same, yet with more features that the array class offers. Note we can sort it, it knows the beginning and end of the array, etc. A **multi-dimensional array**, using the array class is similar to what you would expect. Normally for a 3 row by 4 column array, it would be: *int game[3][4]* to make a 3 row by 4 column hypothetical game. Using the array class it would be: *array<array<int, 4>, 3> arr;* Note row and column are reversed.

126

```cpp
//Simple 3 row by 4 col array
#include<iostream>
#include <string>
#include <array>
using namespace std;

//#define hunters 3
int main()
{
        //an array 3 rows by four cols
        array<array<int, 4>, 3> myarray;

        cout << "Show first row cols: \n";

        for (int position = 0; position < 4; position++)  // 0 -- 3 = 4 columns
        { myarray[0][position] = 0;
        cout << "Current value  row 1 is: " << position << "= col = " << myarray[0][position] << "\n";

          //This will print a zero for each of the positions.
        }

        system("pause");
        return 0;
}
```

The array class is a tad bit different than traditional or native arrays, but not so much. Let's do a bit more with arrays and a new topic they are handy for.

Searching and Sorting

The *algorithm* library include offers the power to perform some searching and sorting operations on a dataset. You certainly could create your own algorithm to do this, and if fact before the library was available, this was the standard process. However modern programming techniques would suggest that the best method for coding would be to at least consider pre-written libraries first. If you have ever head the term "do not reinvent the wheel" this is the general thought.

Two types of searches

There are two types of searches you could do, a *linear* and a *binary*. With a **linear search** you assume the data is not sorted. Since this is the case, you must start from either the beginning or end and just "march" through the data until you find what you are looking for, or report back you cannot find the item in question.

127

With a ***binary search***, the data is sorted, either ascending or descending, such that you can find the midpoint, and determine if your value is above or below the midpoint, once determined you can half the dataset, find the midpoint again, determine if above or below, wash, rinse, repeat! So binary searches, if possible based on whether sorted or now, are very efficient.

```cpp
// Linear search a string
#include <iostream>
#include <string> // for strings and getline
using namespace std;

int main()
{       string my_line="";
        cout << "Enter a line of text with a capital B somewhere.\n";
        getline(cin, my_line);
        cout << "Linear search from start to finish for the B!\n";
        int counter = 0;
        for (char x : my_line)
        {       if (x == 'B')
                        cout << "Found a B here! -> " << counter << "\n";
                else
                        cout << "No B yet\n";
        counter++;
        }
        system("pause");
        return 0;
}
```

The previous examples showed *getline()* which allowed you to enter a sentence, with white space (something *cin* alone will not allow). Also we used an enhanced *for* loop to examine every character, looking for a capital B. Since the sentence is unsorted, we had to use a linear search through every character in the sentence. Next let's try a binary search for data in a simple vector (similar to a single dimensional array).

```cpp
// Binary search ex. 1
#include <iostream>
#include <algorithm>
#include <vector>
using namespace std;

int main()
{
```

```
int data[] = { 1,3,9,2,5,8,7,12 }; //array with data 8 elements 0-7
vector<int> my_vector(data, data + 8); //put into vector and size it
//a vector offers some neat tools
sort(my_vector.begin(), my_vector.end()); // sort the vector

cout << "Is there an 8? \n";
if (binary_search(my_vector.begin(), my_vector.end(), 8))
{
        cout << lower_bound(my_vector.begin(), my_vector.end(), 8) -
        my_vector.begin();
        cout << " <- Found here!\n"; // sub where started from found for 5
} // so 5 is the positio where 8 is in the array!

else
        cout << "Sad, no!\n";

system("pause");
return 0;
}
```

That was fun, but now jot a few notes down for yourself, then try your hand at the learning extension to expand what you have learned.

Notes to remember

Learning extension

1) Take the example we did which allowed the user to only enter five unique values, add in a check for less than 1 or greater than 100, and inform the user. Also keep count of how many attempts are made, regardless of if unique or not and inform the user of this as well.

2) Functionalize the five unique values example. Also if a value not in the range is entered, do not count that loop event. Include all features of #1.

3) The example in the chapter with salespeople totals is not efficient in the end, it needs a loop to handle output of who sold in the ranges. Change it to use a loop.

4) Create a multi-dimensional array for a tic-tac-toe game. You will need to "check" for wins via a loop every time a turn is taken. Allow for two players.

5) Based on #4, allow for random number generation and a user to play against the computer, and (if you are really good….) allow for levels of difficulty where the computer predicts where it should move, based on chances to win, not just open random positions. Create an ASCII board which displays the moves.

6) Add user input for kills and misses to the zombie hunter example. Also allow for more hunters. Be creative and use ASCII art if….you are really good!

7) For the simple 3 row by 4 col array using the array class, add in a second loop so that all rows are displayed neatly. Also make sure you put some data in the elements of the array.

8) Take the example at the end of the chapter on a linear search of a string and allow the user to enter what is searched for.

9) Based on #8, allow for counting of instances of what is searched for. E.g. if you entered several sentences, have it count how many based on number of "." Found.

10) Create a binary search application which is creative, use your imagination!

11) Create a game based on what you learned from this chapter.

12) Create a tutoring or CMI-based (computer managed instruction) application based on what you learned from this chapter.

13) Create a utility application based on what you learned from this chapter.

Chapter 9
Classes and OOP

If you want to have a good understanding of computer programming, you should understand how and why classes are implemented and used. As opposed to an abstract world, the real world is easier to understand for most people. This "real world" is represented in programming by a class (or class template) and classes or "reusable objects" are really the main part of OOP or "Object Oriented Programming". The "objects" are the classes or "nouns" that you will create. Considering all of this, an important consideration when considering classes is its ability to accurately represent the things that make sense to us. This smooths the programming process, helps with debugging, and improves program maintenance. Again, the design and creation of classes is referred to as OOP or *Object Oriented Programming* since "things" such as people, cars, invoices, etc, are objects (which are defined by your class template).

As an example, you design a class which encompasses the behaviors and properties of the thing in question. If it was a person class, then each unique person you created, based on the class template, might have an *age, first name, last name*, etc. Behaviors might be that they could *run, jump, read, shoot zombies,* etc. In programming they would even be referred to as *properties* and *behaviors*. Formally behaviors may well be referred to as *set* and *get* methods which *set* or *get* certain variables in the class. As such, OOP has a few ground rules we need to cover. We noted that the real world is easier to understand than the abstract, so, given that premise, we could say that the real world consists of *entities* and *relationships*. These are really part of a bigger topic called the *entity relationship model*, a topic we will not discuss much further in this text, since it is a rather large topic in and of itself. However, we do need to understand these parts somewhat in order to move forward.

You could think of an *entity* as an object or living thing, or an abstraction of something that could be described by its unique characteristics, similarities, or differences from other entities of the same type. A noun would describe an entity. A person, computer, car, pet, or newspaper, etc. could be an entity. Now, related to classes, a class could be thought of as a template or model that defines the *properties* of an object and also the *methods* it can use (such as a function) to define that object's *behavior.*

You define the properties and methods in a class definition. The object you create that is built from the class is called an *instance* of the class. The design "template" for the class is shared with all objects created from the class, but the unique properties are different. In a nutshell, what an object "knows" is expressed in its properties (data) and what an object can do is defined in the class methods. Identity is how the object is known among other object instances. So, in short consider for OOP an object has state or properties (data), behaviors (functions), and identity for things in it (or how theses things such as variables or functions are known among other objects) e.g. public or private. The last part refers to who can get to what from where which we will get to later.

Along with this, add an *entity set* which is a collection of entities of a similar nature. Your local newspaper might be part of the newspaper entity, a car in the parking lot is part of the parking lot entity, etc. In other words, *an entity is a collection of like items*. Now, in this entity set though, each car in the parking lot is different than the other car in the lot....even though it is true that they are all cars. You get the idea? Think that there are three Mustangs, but each has a unique color, owner, license tag, etc. Got it now? Good! These differences (color? number of doors?) are unique attributes of the similar entities in the entity set.

Classes are not functions, but may contain them

Okay so far? You may still be wondering at this point, "how is this different than a function?" Well, keep in mind we "call" functions over and over, not really creating any new "data types" and in fact with a static class (or class that is just called but you do not create an instance of it, they are the same, but technically beyond that they are different. The value of a variable may change in a function, but no new data types (such as an integer or float) are created. However, with a class, we are creating a compound data type really, based on primitive data types (an integer or double or character would be examples). You are creating your own data type, so to speak with a class. When you create a class, you create one or more new compound variables, your new class, that you can reference, change, and most importantly create new instances (or copies). Just like you can define several variables -- all to be integers -- you can create several objects which are all based on the class you defined. Interestingly enough, they can again contain functions if needed! Excited yet?

Now, to build on the entity and the entity set, we have the *relationship*. This is an association among the members of one or more of your entity sets. Relationships are something you will study in more detail if you have the opportunity to take a database design course. Next, a *relationship set* is a set of related yet unique relationships of the same type. As an example, car size might be regarded as a relationship set between the entity sets of cars and parking lots. The fact that you have email might be seen as a relationship between you, members of an entity set of email users, and your email account, a member of the entity set of your ISP (Internet Service Provider) which hosts your email.

Classes

Objects must be created or "instantiated" based on a class The object is an instance of the class. Most modern languages use classes, so this is an applicable topic for any language you might wish to learn. There is a lot more to it, but let's create a class first in code to see how easy it can be, then we will add more to it. In C++, the authors of the language added an ability to make reusable structures, or objects, known as *classes*. The earlier C language only supported *strucs*, which you read about in a previous chapter and tried your hand at. These are similar to *classes*, but lack control over what can access certain aspects of the structure, or in C++ terms *the object*. Later we will examine this access modifier, known as *public* and *private* access modifiers, but to start let's consider this generic thing, a *struc*(ture).

A *structure* might represent a person, or object, or whatever a noun might represent. In the example below well will see how C++ can use a *struct* to represent a zombie, or vampire. Each structure is a generic template for each of these fictional creatures. So, if you took a template and created many zombies, they might have different numbers of limbs (e.g. some missing), hunger levels, or they may be recently dead or quite stinky being dead for a few weeks or more. Try the example below to see how it works using a *struct* to represent a generic template for things you wish to create (in code only we hope since there are enough zombies around anyway!).

```cpp
// Simple structure

#include <iostream>
using namespace std;
struct zombie
{
        int limbs;   // create attributes which any zombie struct would have
        int hunger_level;
        bool recent_dead;
}; // note semicolon to mark end

int main()  // main part or driver code
{
        zombie sara;  // create a zombie named sara

        sara.hunger_level = 10;  // set her attributes
        sara.limbs = 3;
        sara.recent_dead = 0;

        cout << "Limbs  Hunger Level  Recently Dead as bool" << endl;
        cout << sara.limbs << "\t" << sara.hunger_level << "\t" << sara.recent_dead << endl;

        system("pause");
        return 0;
}
```

Some things to note in the structure example above are that the structure is defined at the top of the same file that also contains the driver code. Also note that the code segment for the structure (and for classes) ends with a semicolon after the closing brace. This is important to note as normally this would result in an error. Try the next example which expands on this example a bit.

```cpp
// More simple structures
#include <iostream>
#include<string>
using namespace std;
struct zombie
{
        int limbs;   // create attributes which any zombie struct would have
        int hunger_level;
        bool recent_dead;
}; // note semicolon to mark end
```

```cpp
struct hunter
{
        string name;  // name of hunter
        int weapons; // how many
        int ammo;
        bool sex; // m=0 female=1

};

int main()
{
        zombie urgha;  // create a zombie named Urgha
        urgha.hunger_level = 10;  // set her attributes
        urgha.limbs = 3;
        urgha.recent_dead = 0;

        hunter smith;
        smith.ammo = 30;
        smith.name = "Smith";
        smith.weapons = 1;
        smith.sex = 1;

        cout << "Limbs  Hunger Level  Recently Dead as bool" << endl;
        cout << urgha.limbs << "\t" << urgh.hunger_level << "\t"
                << urgha.recent_dead << endl;

        cout << "Dispatched by " << smith.name << " he is an " <<
                smith.sex << " male" << "this much ammo: " << smith.ammo << endl;

        system("pause");
        return 0;
}
```

So, in the previous example note that we added two structures, of course though you could have more. In the next and last example of a structure, we will add a function to the struct.

```cpp
// More simple structures
#include <iostream>
#include<string>
using namespace std;
struct zombie
{
        int limbs;  // create attributes which any zombie struct would have
        int hunger_level;
        bool recent_dead;
```

```cpp
};  // note semicolon to mark end

struct hunter
{
        string name;  // name of hunter
        int weapons; // how many
        int ammo;
        bool sex; // m=0 female=1
        void shoot_now()
        {
                cout << "bang bang!!" << " the struct did a function!\n\n" ;
        }

};

int main()
{
        zombie urgha;  // create a zombie named Urgha
        urgha.hunger_level = 10;  // set her attributes
        urgha.limbs = 3;
        urgha.recent_dead = 0;

        hunter smith;
        smith.ammo = 30;
        smith.name = "Smith";
        smith.weapons = 1;
        smith.sex = 1;

        cout << "Limbs  Hunger Level  Recently Dead as bool" << endl;
        cout << urgha.limbs << "\t" << urgha.hunger_level << "\t"
                << urgha.recent_dead << endl;

        cout << "Dispatched by " << smith.name << " he is an " <<
                smith.sex << " male" << "this much ammo: " << smith.ammo << endl;

        cout << "\nHere comes a zombie towards us!\n\n";

        smith.shoot_now();// call the shoot now function

        system("pause");
        return 0;
}
```

So, we are going to move on next to classes, which are very similar to structures. The big difference is *structures* are inherently *public* by nature and classes are by default *private*, but classes will in fact be both in practical application. With *strucs* you have no *private* access modifier. Also, classes will, as you see describe things, like nouns do in English, and really a class is designed to offer something to an interface. Both do offer abstraction of implementation details though and both can and should be used as appropriate. Next let's get started with classes!

Class design is central to concept of Object Oriented Programming

When you are considering a class design, consider that some things (variables or functions) may need to be hidden from the public interface (the driver part of the code). Keywords *public* and *private* are used to note things that the driver can get to or that are only accessible from **within** the class and not from the driver. What follows is a simple and open class where the driver can get to anything.

```cpp
// C++ first one file simple class
#include <iostream>
using namespace std;
class zombie
{
public:
        int limbs;
        int hunger_level;
        //display welcome message
        void displayMessage() const // constant function
        {
                cout << "\t\tWelcome to Zombieland!\n\a\n\a" << endl;
        }
        void showMe()  // function
        {
                cout << "I like the undead!!\n\n";
        }

};  // note semicolon!
int main()
{
        zombie myZombie;
        myZombie.limbs = 4;
        myZombie.hunger_level = 8;
        myZombie.displayMessage();
        cout << "Hunger level is " << myZombie.hunger_level << "\n";
        myZombie.showMe();
```

137

```cpp
        system("pause");
        return 0;

}
```

Next let's hide something from the driver (*and note the error*) and fix it in a subsequent program which will show a proper way to access something private from a public interface.

```cpp
// C++ first one file simple class that fails due to private section
#include <iostream>
using namespace std;

class zombie
{
public:
        int limbs;
        int hunger_level;
        //display welcome message
        void displayMessage() const // constant function
        {   cout << "\t\tWelcome to Zombieland!\n\a\n\a" << endl;
        }

private:
        void showMe()  // function
        {   cout << "I like the undead!!\n\n";
        }
};

int main()
{
        zombie myZombie;
        myZombie.limbs = 4;
        myZombie.hunger_level = 8;
        myZombie.displayMessage();
        cout << "Hunger level is " << myZombie.hunger_level << "\n";
        myZombie.showMe();

        system("pause");
        return 0;
}
```

Note that if using Visual Studio, the ShowMe function in int main() shows an error as it should. Next let's fix it.

```cpp
// C++ first one file simple class
#include <iostream>
using namespace std;

class zombie
{
public:
        int limbs;
        int hunger_level;
        //display welcome message
        void displayMessage() const // constant function
        {
                cout << "\t\tWelcome to Zombieland!\n\a\n\a" << endl;
        }
        void call_show_me()
        {
                cout << "calling function now....\n";
                showMe();  // put void in front of this and nothing happens!
        }
private:
        void showMe()  // function
        {
                cout << "I like the undead tons!!\n\n";
        }
};
int main()
{
        zombie myZombie;
        myZombie.limbs = 4;
        myZombie.hunger_level = 8;
        myZombie.displayMessage();
        cout << "Hunger level is " << myZombie.hunger_level << "\n\n";
        myZombie.call_show_me();

        system("pause");
        return 0;
}
```

Since *call_show_me()* is public, it can call a private function or variable. Next we will look at *set* and *get* methods.

Set and Get

As you may have surmised, set will set a variable, in our case one that is private, and get will give you access to private data. The names *get* and *set* are not syntax-related but explain what they do, so stay with them for clarity. Use them for input validation (e.g. a value is in a range) or number or length of a variable, etc.

```cpp
// C++ first use of set methods in class
#include <iostream>
#include <string>
using namespace std;

class zombie
{
public:
        //display welcome message
        void set_name(string zname)
        {
                name = zname;
        }
        void set_hunger(int value)
        {
                if (value > 0 && value < 11)
                        hunger_level = value;
                else
                {       cout << "Value not in valid range, setting to 0";
                        hunger_level = 0;
                }
        }
        void show_data()  // shows private data
        {
                cout << "Name: " << name << endl;
                cout << "hunger level:  " << hunger_level  << endl;
        }

private:
        string name;
        int hunger_level;
};

int main()
{
        zombie myZombie;
        cout << "Enter zombie name : ";
```

```cpp
        string aName;
        int level;
        cin >> aName;
        myZombie.set_name(aName);
        cout << "Enter hunger level 1 - 10\n";
        cin >> level;
        myZombie.set_hunger(level);
        myZombie.show_data();
        system("pause");
        return 0;
}
```

Let's try a bit more with *get* and *set*.

```cpp
#include <iostream>
#include <string>
using namespace std;

class worker
{
public:
        float hourly_pay;
        int years_service;

        void set_name(string worker_name)
        {
                last_name = worker_name;
        }

        void show_weekly_pay()
        {
                cout << "Name: " << last_name << " made " << hourly_pay << endl;
                cout << "They have worked for " << years_service << " years" << endl;
                cout << "They made $" << weekly << " this week\n\n\n";
        }
        void compute(int hours)
        {
                if (hours > 0)
                        cout << "great job this week!";
                else
                {       "invalid hours, setting to 1\n";
                hours = 1;
                }

                weekly = hourly_pay * hours;
        }
private:
```

```cpp
        string last_name;
        float weekly;
};

int main()
{
        worker worker_1;
        cout << "Enter last name: ";
        string w_name;
        cin >> w_name;
        worker_1.set_name(w_name);
        int years;
        cout << "Enter years: \n";
        cin >> years;
        worker_1.years_service = years;
        cout << "How many hours did they work this week: " << endl;
        int hours;
        cin >> hours;
        cout << "\nHow much do they get paid per hour? " << endl;
        cin >> worker_1.hourly_pay;
        worker_1.compute(hours);
        worker_1.show_weekly_pay();
        system("pause");
        return 0;
}
```

Next, let's add two classes in. They will be separate from each other (for now). Could you have more, sure! Let your imagination and needs fly on class design.

```cpp
//Two classes on one program example
#include <iostream>
#include <string>
using namespace std;

class worker_hourly
{
public:
        float hourly_pay;
        int years_service;

        void set_name(string worker_name)
        {
                last_name = worker_name;
        }

        void show_weekly_pay()
```

```cpp
        {
                cout << "Name: " << last_name << " made " << hourly_pay << endl;
                cout << "They have worked for " << years_service  << " years" << endl;
                cout << "They made $" << weekly << " this week\n\n\n";
        }
        void compute(int hours)
        {
                if (hours > 0)
                        cout << "great job this week!";
                else
                {       "invalid hours, setting to 1\n";
                hours = 1;
                }

                weekly = hourly_pay * hours;
        }
private:
        string last_name;
        float weekly;
};
class salary_worker
{
private:
        int salary;
public:
        void set_salary(int sal)
        {       salary = sal;    }

        int get_salary()
        {       return salary; }
};

int main()
{
        worker_hourly worker_1;
        cout << "Enter last name: ";
        string w_name;
        cin >> w_name;
        worker_1.set_name(w_name);
        int years;
        cout << "Enter years: \n";
        cin >> years;
        worker_1.years_service = years;
        cout << "How many hours did they work this week: " << endl;
        int hours;
        cin >> hours;
```

```cpp
    cout << "\nHow much do they get paid per hour? " << endl;
    cin >> worker_1.hourly_pay;
    worker_1.compute(hours);
    worker_1.show_weekly_pay();

    cout << "How much do salary employees make per year? \n";
    int their_salary;
    cin >> their_salary;
    salary_worker salary_person;
    salary_person.set_salary(their_salary);
    cout << "Salary folks make " << salary_person.get_salary() << endl;

    system("pause");
    return 0;
}
```

Note that we used proper form and provided *get* and *set* methods. Could there have been more input validation, you bet, but it does show how things work though a bit.

Inheritance

Another handy feature of OOP is the concept of inheritance. Just like it sounds, classes can be joined such that one class can "inherit" features (variables or functions) from other classes. Sound koolo? It is! In the next example consider that any object such as a zombie or a vampire would be undead, so in our example both of these things would inherit from a base or parent class things common to them all. In our case both are undead folks. But just like when you inherit things from your parents, such as skin color, eye color, etc. you also have unique attributes, so in this next example even though we have a zombie, which is undead, he (Fred) has a unique name, that we change to Bill.

```cpp
#include <iostream>
#include <string>
using namespace std;

class undead //base or super class to inherit from
{
public:
        string type="Undead folks\n";
};
```

```cpp
class zombie : public undead // sub class or child class inheriting from base
{
public:
        string name = "Fred the green zombie\n";
        void set_name(string new_name)
        {
                name = new_name;
        }
};

//main function
int main()
{       zombie fred;  //undead variables and functions are seen by sub class

        cout << fred.type; // print base class variable
        cout << fred.name; // print child class variable

        cout << "Change Freds name\n";
        fred.set_name("Bill");
        cout << "New name for Fred is now:  " << fred.name << endl;

        system("pause");
        return 0;
}
```

In the next example you are creating a base weapons class, with other classes of specific weapons which inherit from the base or parent class.

```cpp
#include <iostream>
#include <string>
using namespace std;

class weapon //parent class
{
public:
        string type = "weapon\n";
};

class rifle : public weapon // child class
{
public:
        string name = "A rifle is good zombie medicine\n";
        void set_name(string new_name)
```

```cpp
        {
                name = new_name;
        }
};

class crossbow : public weapon
{
public:
        string name = "A crossbow does not make much noise!\n";
        void set_name(string type)
        {
                name = type;
        }
};

int main()
{
        weapon zeds_weapons;
        rifle zeds_rifle;
        cout << zeds_weapons.type;
        cout << zeds_rifle.name << " is Zed's rifle\n";
        crossbow zeds_cross;
        cout << zeds_cross.name << "  is also a " << zeds_cross.type << endl;
        // note type is in weapon class but was inherited by the crossbow class

        system("pause");
        return 0;
}
```

Well that finishes this chapter, but there is much more to learn about class design and OOP in chapter 10. Try the learning examples then continue to the next chapter for more.

Notes to remember

Learning extension

1) Create a structure for a car or truck and display the results to the screen.

2) Create a structure for a pet and display results to the screen.

3) Create a fun program with three structures. Allow for user data input to the variables and display the results to the screen.

4) Create a structure which allows for user input and validation (such as length of input, etc.) and allow the user to re-enter improper data.

5) Create a class and driver (in one file) with no explicit constructor. Class should have a public function which displays "Hello World".

6) Create a class and driver (in two files) with no explicit constructor. Class should have a public function which displays "Hello World".

7) Create a pet tracking program with get and set methods. Provide age validation which insures greater than age 0 and less than 100. Provide at least three get and set methods with private variables in the class and a show data function.

8) Create a program with get and set methods that computes monthly pay, .07% tax withholding, and net take-home pay after taxes. Allow the user to input monthly pay and provide input validation and a show data function.

9) Add a function which increases pay by 10% to #8.

10) On the two class example with salary_worker, add in other features for a salary worker and provide input validation such that the salary per year is a positive value. If you are really good add an option to only input monthly salary for them, and have it compute this by 12 months for yearly salary. If you are very good allow for tax of .07% per monthly pay period (only if you are very good though!).

11) Create an application for pets, with parent and child classes.

12) Re-write the hourly and salary employee example to use inheritance. How is this better than the example in the chapter?

13) Create a useful application with classes for someone you know or a worthy social cause.

14) Create a base and sub class for vehicles. Do not search the Internet for examples!

15) For the weapons class example, add set and get methods, set some variables as private, and perhaps even add another class (a derived class).

Chapter 10

Constructors, Inheritance, Friend and Protected, and Templates

So, for now when you have designed a class, there was an implicit *constructor* which "constructed" the instance of the object from the class you were creating. There was nothing you had to type. However, there may well be times when you want to pass some data to a class such as an initial name or some data value like a date or time. Explicit constructors, which you will write handle this. Compared to a function they are the same except that there is no return data type and they are only called automatically when you create an instance of an object. You will not call a constructor over and over as you might with a function. Consider the next simple example to see an explicit constructor in action.

```cpp
#include <iostream>
using namespace std;

class account
{ private:
        int account_number = 0;
public:
        account::account(int your_account)//constructor
        {
                set_acct(your_account);
        };
        ;
        void set_acct(int new_acct)
        {
                cout << "Account created!\n";
                account_number = new_acct;
        }
        void get_acct()
        {
                cout << "Account # is: " << account_number << endl;
        }
};

int main()
{
        account smith(100001);  //create one
        smith.get_acct(); // show acct #
```

148

```
        system("pause");
        return 0;
}
```

So, in the aforementioned simple example a hypothetical bank is creating a new account for Smith. The information that is required would be an account number, in this case 100001. The constructor (which has a class specifier ***account::account***) calls a set method to set a private variable. The class specifier will be important in few pages when we get to multi-part class files. No input validation was performed, though it could have been. Lastly our *get* method just did something, though it could have returned a value back. Simple right? Let's add to it.

```
//Bank Account with two arguement constructor
#include <iostream>
using namespace std;

class account
{
private:
        int account_number = 0;
        int balance = 0;

public:
        account::account(int your_account, int your_balance)//constructor
        {
                set_acct(your_account);
                set_balance(your_balance);
        }

        void set_acct(int new_acct)
        {
                cout << "Account created!\n";
                account_number = new_acct;
        }
        void set_balance(int initial_balance)
        {
                if (initial_balance > 0)  //input validation
                {
                        cout << "Deposit made to new account.\n";
                        balance = initial_balance;
                }
                else
                        cout << "Deposit not valid!\n";
```

```cpp
        }

        void get_acct()
        {
                cout << "Account # is: " << account_number << endl;
                cout << "Balance is: " << balance << endl;
        }
};

int main()
{
        account smith(1122345, 5000);  //create acct and deposit $5000
        smith.get_acct(); // show acct #

        system("pause");
        return 0;
}
```

In the previous example note that there are two arguments required for the constructor now. Also note that a bit of *input validation* was added so that if a user entered a negative balance it would not accept it. Typically *set* methods would be used for something like this, else you could just set the variables directly. Next let's deconstruct an object as well to release it from memory or do some termination housekeeping.

```cpp
// Bank Account with two arguement constructor
// does not really remove from memory but erases data
#include <iostream>
using namespace std;

class account
{
private:
        int account_number = 0;
        int balance = 0;

public:
        account(int, int);
        ~account();
        void set_acct(int);
        void set_balance(int);
        void get_acct();
};
```

```cpp
account::account(int your_account, int your_balance) //constructor
    {
            set_acct(your_account);
            set_balance(your_balance);
    }
    account::~account()  //destructor
    {
            cout << "Account closed!\n";
            account_number = 0;
            balance = 0;
    }

    void account::set_acct(int new_acct)
    {
            cout << "Account created!\n";
            account_number = new_acct;
    }
    void account::set_balance(int initial_balance)
    {
            if (initial_balance > 0)  //input validation
            {
                    cout << "Deposit made to new account.\n";
                    balance = initial_balance;
            }
            else
                    cout << "Deposit not valid!\n";
    }

    void account::get_acct()
    {
            cout << "Account # is: " << account_number << endl;
            cout << "Balance is: " << balance << endl;
    }

int main()
{
        account smith(1122345, 5000);  //create acct and deposit $5000
        smith.get_acct(); // show acct #

        smith.~account();

        smith.get_acct(); // prove it is gone
        system("pause");
        return 0;
}
```

Okay, don't jump in the zombie pit yet, it was big code for sure. But, a destructor (same name as constructor but with a tilde (~) was added to clear things out with done. In this case it is still in memory but cleared for our purposes. Next, we are technically setup for multi-part files now. The first part of your code was the prototype of things to happen (note only int was listed and not the variable name). Then after the semi colon, we provided function definitions with specific details and names. Also note the class was listed first followed by double colons and the function name. Whew! Big code, and ugly. Soon we will put this in separate files and it will be nice and organized yet do the same thing! But first a bit more on basic class design.

How to share a variable in a class with all class instances

Would it not be neat to have all class instances share a bit of information? E.g. they all knew how many had been created, or scores were shared between player objects? You bet this is handy! Try it out.

```
// Example of shared static variable
//count shows how many bank accounts total
#include <iostream>
using namespace std;
//shared variable known to all class instances
static int number_of_accounts=0; // start at 0

class account
{
private:
        int account_number = 0;
public:
        account(int);
        void set_acct(int);
        void get_acct();

};

account::account(int your_account)
        {
                set_acct(your_account);
                number_of_accounts += 1;
        }

        void account::set_acct(int new_acct)
        {
```

```
                cout << "Account created!\n";
                account_number = new_acct;
        }

        void account::get_acct()
        {
                cout << "Account # is: " << account_number << endl;
                cout << "Nothing else but how many accounts " << number_of_accounts << endl;
        }

int main()
{
        account smith(1122345);
        smith.get_acct(); // show info -- one account

        account brown(101);
        smith.get_acct(); // show info but now two accounts

        system("pause");
        return 0;
}
```

So, the previous example shows a variable that all instances derived from the class can update and read. In other words a *shared* or *common variable*, in this case showing how many. Let's next examine other access specifiers such as *protected* and *friend*. Remember that from chapter 7 variables live out their happy lives in a memory location in RAM. The location is assigned by the compiler based on a free area, or an area where nothing is already stored, such as a running program. As such it is will vary over time, which is why when you run the next example on different computers, or the same one at different times, the address location will change.

For many of the previous chapters we have addressed variables directly, e.g. **cout << tax** would return the data stored in the memory location for tax. Easy enough. However as noted in chapter 7, there are times when it might be nice to point to a memory location of a variable from another location (a *pointer*) which you could think is similar to a *shortcut*. Also, it might be nice to know the *memory address* of a variable, the *address of operator*. Both are easy to use and might come in handy. Try the next example to see them in action.

```cpp
#include <iostream>
using namespace std;

int main()
{
        int foo = 9;
        cout << foo << " what is stored in foo\n";
        //address of operator
        cout << &foo << " memory address of foo\n";
        //create a pointer to foo
        int *ptrfoo = &foo;
        cout << *ptrfoo << " a pointer to foo variable"<< endl;

        system("pause");
        return 0;
}
```

So, the **&** symbol preceding a variable denotes a memory address and the * symbol denotes a pointer. Nothing else is needed to get this to work!

Friend functions

Private members of a class are only accessible by the class itself. However, something, in this case a function, designated as a *friend*, can access it! How cool is that? Try it and see.


```cpp
//Friend function example
#include <iostream>
using namespace std;

class space
{
private:
        int area;
public:
        space()
        { area = 0; }
        //make add_one a friend function
        friend int add_one(space);
}; // class ends

// friend function definition, note not a class but a func.
int add_one(space x) // not the space x flight firm!
{
```

154

```
        //access private variable
        //note it is private but since it is a friend can access
        x.area += 1;
        return x.area;
}

int main()
{
        space my_area;
        cout << "space: " << add_one(my_area) << endl;

        system("pause");
        return 0;
}
```

Add_one was made a *friend* and thus given access to the private variable. Next and last let's consider *protected*.

Protected and derived classes

A class that **derives or inherits features** from a base or parent class can get to items flagged as *protected*. They cannot access *private*, but sometimes an intermediary access such as *protected* is nice. So, *public* is wide open, *private* only to the original class, and *protected* is available if it is a derived class. Note the next example which shows this. Also, uncomment the section noted to see an access violation.


```
// Protected members can be accessed from derived classes.
#include<iostream>
using namespace std;

class base_class {

private:
        int a_private_var = 1;
protected:
        int a_protected_var = 2;
public:
        int a_public_var = 3;
};

class derived : base_class // this inherits from the base class its features
{
```

```cpp
public:
        int return_protected()
        {
                return a_protected_var;
        }
        int return_public()
        {
                return a_public_var;
        }
        //int return_public()  // uncomment to produce error
        //{
        //        return a_private_var;
        //}

};

class non_derived  // can only get to public since not derived
{
private:
        base_class B;  // create instance so we can get to it
public:
        int get_public()
        {
                return B.a_public_var;
        }
};

int main()
{
        cout << "\tExamples of derived and non-derieved classes with protected status\n\n";
        derived my_base_1; // create derived class
        cout << "base 1-> " << my_base_1.return_protected() << " is a protected variable!\n";
        cout << "base 1-> " << my_base_1.return_public() << " is a public variable!\n";
        non_derived sample;  // create non-derived class
        cout << "non-derived public var " << sample.get_public() << " Non-derived can only get
to public\n\n";

        system("pause");
        return 0;
}
```

Many of your programs will be fine with just *public* and *private*, however for advanced work
you many find *friend* and *protected* status to offer some advantages. Next let's examine multi-

part class files which will make things a bit easier to manage when your file size (e.g. line count) gets large.

Multi-part class files

Separate class from implementation via separate file for class header and prototypes

So, you can only imagine that with a very few classes your programs could be messy in a hurry. If you implement the "work" a class does into separate files, knows and "header files" and "function prototype" files (similar to what we did with functions) you can make your code much easier to read and debug. Other zombie hunters reading your code will thank you for this kindness in cleaner design.

For the next simple example, you will create three files in your empty C++ project. The first will be a header file, that will have the same name (not extension) as one of the CPP files. These are the function prototype file and function definition files. The first is a general summary of the functions, only what they take or give back to the calling functions. The second defines exactly how the functions work. The names must be the same as the header file is included as a manual local library include (noted not with alligators <> but with " ". Of course all files should be in the same folder. The last and final third file can have any valid name but is the actual driver code, has int main() and does the real work. This next one has just one simple function. Try it with three files and run to see how it works.

```cpp
//header file simple.h   part 1 of 3
#include <string>
using namespace std;

class simple
{
public:
        void show_stats();

private:
        string hunter_name="Fred the Z hunter";
};
```

```cpp
//function prototype file
//simple.cpp part 2 of 3
#include <string>
#include "simple.h"
using namespace std;

void simple::show_stats()
{
        cout << "Name of hunter is: " << hunter_name << endl;
}

//zombie hunter driver
//driver.cpp  part 3 of 3
#include <iostream>
#include "simple.h"
using namespace std;

int main()
{
        simple Fred;

        Fred.show_stats();

        system("pause");
        return 0;
}
```

Of course you can have more than three, but there will be only one driver. This last example was just a simple start to get you warmed up and on target. Next let's consider a larger and full-featured example. This one also features an explicit constructor.

```cpp
//header file 1 of 3  file name = zombie_hunter.h
#include <string>
using namespace std;
class zombie_hunter
{
public:
        zombie_hunter(string);  // constructor prototype
        void set_age(int);
        void show_stats();
        void set_weapon(string);
private:
        string hunter_name;
        int hunter_age;
        string weapon;   };
```

```cpp
//function definition file 2 of 3
//zombie_hunter.cpp
#include <iostream>
#include <string>
#include "zombie_hunter.h"
using namespace std;
//explicit constructor
zombie_hunter::zombie_hunter(string name)
{
        hunter_name = name;
}
void zombie_hunter::set_age(int age)
{
        hunter_age = age;
}
void zombie_hunter::show_stats()
{
        cout << "Name of hunter is: " << hunter_name << "age" << hunter_age;
        cout << "\nHe uses a: " << weapon;
}
void zombie_hunter::set_weapon(string myweapon)
{
        weapon = myweapon;
}


//zombie hunter driver part 3 of 3
//zdriver.cpp
#include <iostream>
#include "zombie_hunter.h"
using namespace std;
int main()
{       zombie_hunter Fred("Mean Fred");
        zombie_hunter Barney("Bam Bam");
        Fred.set_age(50);
        Fred.set_weapon("axe");
        Barney.set_age(22);
        Barney.set_weapon("CETME .308 with Trijicon sight");
        Fred.show_stats();
        Barney.show_stats();
        system("pause");
        return 0;
}
```

Overloaded constructors in multi-part files

In the next example, consider two different explicit constructors. They both have the same name, but depending on how they are instantiated a different constructor is called.

```cpp
// A simple three-file class and driver with overloaded constructors
//there are two, with the one chosen by the number of arguments given
//e.g. give it a value, that constructor with requires a value is chosen, otherwise
//give it no values and the other is chosen.
//crypto currencey!!!!   crypto.h

class crypto
{
private:
        int value;
public:
        crypto();  //overloaded explicit constructor prototypes
        crypto(int);

        void set_value(int);

        void get_value();

};

//Crypto currency
//crypto.cpp
#include <iostream>
#include "crypto.h"
using namespace std;

crypto::crypto() {
        value = 1; // default value
}
crypto::crypto(int mkt_value)
{
        value = mkt_value;
        cout << "Private variable value for crypto currencty now set to " << mkt_value << endl;
}
void crypto::set_value(int init_value)
{
        if (init_value > 0)
                value = init_value;
}

void crypto::get_value()
{
```

```cpp
        cout << "Value of this crypto currency is: " << value << endl;
}

//Crypto currency driver
//blockchaindriver.cpp
#include <iostream>
using namespace std;
#include "crypto.h"

int main()
{
        crypto dodge_coin;   // calls the first crypto constructor
        crypto bitcoin(1000); // second crypto constructor

        cout << "\t\tHere is our crypto currency!\n";

        dodge_coin.get_value();
        bitcoin.get_value();


        system("pause");

        return 0;
}
```

Next, let's consider a zombie gradebook (zombies go to school too right?) named *zgradebook*.

```cpp
//file 1 header
///zgradebook.h
#include <iostream>
#include <string>
using namespace std;

class zgradebook
{
public:
        zgradebook(string);

        void zgradebook::set_name(string);

        void zgradebook::displayMessage() const;

        string zgradebook::get_name()
        {
        return zname;
        }
```

```cpp
private:
        string zname;  };


//zgradebook function definitions file 2
//zgradebook.cpp
#include <iostream>
#include "zgradebook.h"
using namespace std;

zgradebook::zgradebook(string name)
{
        set_name(name);
}

void zgradebook::set_name(string the_name)
{
        if (the_name.length() > 1)
        {
                cout << "Name set\n";
                zname = the_name;
        }
        else
        {
                cout << "Name too short or missing";
                zname = "null";
        }
}

void zgradebook::displayMessage() const
        {
                cout << "Welcome to the Zombie Grade Book!" << endl;
        }


//zombie gradebook driver
//zgradedriver.cpp
//file 3 of 3 driver zombie gradebook
#include <iostream>
#include "zgradebook.h"
using namespace std;

int main()
{
        zgradebook blankgradebook2("Fred the Zombie!\n\n");
```

```
cout << blankgradebook2.get_name() << endl;

system("pause");

return 0;
```

}

Dealing with people, such as perhaps an HR program is very real-world. Next let's work with a person class. Put the classes in their files, and the driver in another, all four in the same project. Note in the header there is more than summary information, and note that we have inheritance in this. A zombie or employee is also a person or at least was!

```
//file 1 Person.h   note a header file!
class Person
{
private:
    string Name;
    int Age;

public:
    Person(string strName, int nAge)
    {
        Name = strName;
        Age = nAge;
    }

    string GetName()
      {
        return Name;
      }

    void setName(string newName)
    {
        Name=newName;
    }

    int GetAge()
      { return Age; }

};
```

```
//put this in a file named Employee.h
//file 2

class Employee
{
private:
    string m_strEmployer;

public:
    Employee(string strEmployer)
        : m_strEmployer(strEmployer)
    {  cout << "Welcome to Umbrella Corp!\n\n";      }

    string GetEmployer()
       {
       return m_strEmployer;
       }
};

// Zombie publicly inherits Person and Employee
// this in a file named Zombie.h file 3
class Zombie : public Person, public Employee
{
private:
    int m_nZombieGrade;

public:
    Teacher(string strName, int nAge, string strEmployer, int nZombieGrade)
        : Person(strName, nAge), Employee(strEmployer), m_nZombieGrade(nZombieGrade)
    {  // note format is same as Person  Name=strName; and Person
        // Age = nAge;  // etc etc.      }
};

// part 4 driver file
#include<string>
#include<iostream>
usingnamespace std;
#include "Person.h"
#include "Employee.h"
#include "Zombie.h"

int main()
{
    Zombie smith("Jim B. Smith",46,"Woods Hill" ,2);

    cout << "Name is " << smith.GetName() << "\n";
```

```
        // add set and get methods where missing
        // create only a person object
        //create only an employee object
        //create a second zombie object
        system("pause" );

    return 0;
```

Could the aforementioned example have a summary header file and subsequent definition file, you bet! However, since it was pretty short, and there were three classes that part was unnecessary overhead. Good though, now that you have this one working, add set and get methods, create non-derived instances, create just an employee, and create and modify a second zombie object.   In the next example, consider an accounting program for Umbrella Corportation. It has three parts and has an explicit constructor with two arguments.

```
//file 1 header prototypes
// account.h
#include<string>
using namespace std;

class account
{
public:
        account(string, int);  // explicit constructor..just

        void getBalance();

        void setCredit(int);

private:
        string cust_acct_number;
        int balance = 0;

};

//file 2 function definitions
#include<iostream>
#include<string>
#include "account.h"
using namespace std;
```

```cpp
account::account(string acct_number, int init_balance)
{
        cust_acct_number = acct_number;

        if (init_balance >= 0)
        {
                balance = init_balance;
        }
        else
        {
                cout << "Balance less than 0, defaulting to 0";
                balance = 0;
        }
}
        void account::getBalance()
        {
                cout << balance << " is your current balance." << endl;
        }

        void account::setCredit(int add_to) // add to account balance
        {
                balance += add_to;

        }

//file 3 driver
#include<iostream>
#include<string>
#include "account.h"
using namespace std;

int main()
{
        string ac_name;
        int bal;

        cout << "Please enter account number: ";
        cin >> ac_name;

        cout << "Enter initial balance: ";
        cin >> bal;

        account jbbaccount(ac_name, bal);

        jbbaccount.getBalance();
```

166

```
cout << "Enter amount to add to balance: ";
int add;
cin >> add;

jbbaccount.setCredit(add);

jbbaccount.getBalance();

system("pause");
return 0;    }
```

Well, now that the finances for our global company are in good order, let's consider persistent data or data that exists after your program is removed from memory. A review of chapter 7 will show you how to write data to files if you forgot (and hopefully you did not!). Lastly, let's examine some generic structures which are similar, yet different than overloaded operators. Templates can allow some flexibility in data types used. Read on for more.

Function templates

A function template is a generic structure that works with different data types. If you give it a character, integer, etc. it behaves in a similar fashion. Try the simple example which follows to see it in action.

```
//template max returns the maximum of the two elements
#include<iostream>
using namespace std;

template <class M>
M max(M a, M b)
{
        if (a > b)
                return a;
        else
                return b;
}

int main()
{
        cout << "First integers compared" << endl;
        cout << "max of 2 and 10:  " << max(2, 10) << "\n\n";
        cout << "Next characters compared\n";
        cout << "max('z', 'h') = " << max('z', 'h') << endl;
        cout << "Consult an ASCII table for decimal values for chars for comparison!\n";
```

```
        system("pause");
        return 0;
}
```

Well that finished the chapter and the text. If you feel there is more to learn, yes there is my young apprentice! You should be ready to learn at this point, you are ready to continue your journey. I sincerely hope it is a happy one. Life if short, time precious. Enjoy every moment, help others, do your best work.

Thank you and I wish you the best.

Burton

Notes to remember

Learning extension

1) For the Bank Account class with two arguments, add a third string argument for account holder name, provide get and set methods for it as well. Also add debit and credit methods to set and get funds to the balance.

2) Change what you did for #1 above to allow the user to purchase an item but check their balance first to see if they have enough money. If not tell them how much they have in the account.

3) Create a POS (point of sale) class and driver with class arguments including sub total of bill, tip percentage, and customer name. Class should produce a final total, dollar amount for tip, sub total, customer name, and name of waiter/waitress. Display using fun ASCII art with business name at top (if you are *really* good!)

4) Create a header, class definition, and driver (three files) with no explicit constructor. Class should have a public function which displays "Hello World".

5) Create a header, class definition, and driver (three files) with an explicit constructor. Class should have a public function which displays "Hello xxxx" where xxxx is a word used as part of the instantiation string for the class object. Allow user input of a string. Include private variables as well.

* For the following allow for get and set, error control, etc. Use professional techniques and do not short-change your coding.

6) Create a pet class using three part files.

7) Create an auto policy class using three part files.

8) Create a zombie insurance class. You want to be able to insure your zombie right?

9) Create a new and improved bank account class with a static variable for number of accounts and a protected or friend class as well.

10) Create an undead class.

11) Create a zombie hunter weapons class.

12) Create a student class.

13) Create an hourly, weekly, and salary worker pay class. Allow for overtime if over 40 hours if hourly. Use derived classes.

14) Create a vehicle class.

15) Create a music class with various artists and genres. Use derived classes.

16) Create a spaceship or alien class.

17) Demonstrate an innovative use of the *friend* function.

18) Demonstrate an innovative use of *protected*.

19) Add functions to the zombie grade book. Use your imagination.

20) Add features to the accounting program.

21) Add another type of undead besides zombies to the example (perhaps a vampire class).